From Your Friends At The MAILBOX®

JANUARY

A MONTH OF REPRODUCIBLES AT YOUR FINGERTIPS!

Project Editor:
Mary Lester

Editor:
Darcy Brown

Writers:
Darcy Brown, Rebecca Brudwick, Kimberly Fields, Cynthia Holcomb, Nicole Iacovazzi, Mary Lester

Art Coordinator:
Clevell Harris

Artists:
Pam Crane, Nick Greenwood, Clevell Harris, Susan Hodnett, Sheila Krill, Rob Mayworth, Kimberly Richard, Donna K. Teal

Cover Artist:
Jennifer L. Tipton

ISBN #1-56234-290-8

Manufactured in the United States

10 9 8 7 6 5 4 3 2 1

Table Of Contents

Name ____________________

January Free Time

Monday	Tuesday	Wednesday	Thursday	Friday
Happy Birthday, Betsy Ross! Born on January 1, 1752, Betsy helped make the first United States flag. Design and draw a flag for your city.	It's time to make your resolutions for the new year! List five or more things you want to do this year.	Alaska became the 49th state on January 3, 1959. Research and write four facts about this large northern state.	January is National Eye Care Month. Draw a picture of yourself wearing a snazzy pair of glasses.	Read *The Legend Of Old Befana* (Harcourt Brace & Company, 1980) by Tomie dePaola. Learn about an old woman who leaves gifts for children on January 6.
Does your desk need cleaning? National Clean-Off-Your-Desk Day is the second Monday in January. Don't forget to clean the inside of your desk, too!	Secret Pal Day is the second Sunday in January. Write a paragraph describing a nice thing that you might do for a secret pal.	Write the number of days left in this month. Add your age to that number. Subtract the number of fingers on your left hand. Write the answer.	Banana Split Day is January 11. Draw a picture of your favorite ice creams and toppings in a fancy dish.	January is National Soup Month. List every type of soup you have tried. Put a star beside your favorite one. Put a triangle beside your least favorite one.
National Hobby Month is observed in January. Write a paragraph about your favorite hobby or one you would like to have.	Amelia Earhart became the first woman to fly alone across the Pacific Ocean in January 1935. List five things you would take on a long airplane trip.	Martin Luther King, Jr., was born on January 15, 1929. Dr. King worked peacefully to get equal rights for all people. Write about a peaceful way to solve a problem.	Pooh Day is January 18. A. A. Milne, the author of the Winnie-the-Pooh series, was born on this day in 1882. List and draw characters found in these books.	Hats off to you! Hat Day is the third Friday in January. Draw a picture of a goofy hat.
The first basketball game was played in January 1892 at a YMCA. Design and color a new basketball uniform.	January 23 is National Handwriting Day. Write a thank-you note to your teacher in your very best handwriting.	Super Bowl® Sunday is in January. List all the sports you can think of that use a ball.	National Puzzle Day is January 29. Draw a picture and cut it into puzzle-shaped pieces. Ask a classmate to put it back together.	Look at today's date. How many days are left in the year? Show your work on a sheet of paper. (Remember, there are 365 days in a year!)

Note To The Teacher: Have each student staple a copy of this page inside a file folder. Direct students to store their completed work in their folders.

Name ____________________

January
Events And Activities For The Family

Directions: Select at least one activity below to complete as a family by the end of January. *(Challenge: See if your family can complete all three activities.)*

Poetry Break

Take a break and read some poetry during January. Make the poetry break extra special by asking family members to read aloud some of their favorite poetry. Gather books of poems, such as those listed, for the younger family members. Your family will rave about taking a poetry break!

Lots Of Limericks
Selected by Myra Cohn Livingston
Illustrated by Rebecca Perry
Margaret K. McElderry Books, 1991

The New Kid On The Block
Written by Jack Prelutsky
Illustrated by James Stevenson
Greenwillow Books, 1984

A Light In The Attic
Written and Illustrated by Shel Silverstein
Harper & Row, Publishers, Inc.; 1981

Breakfast Treat

What better time is there to observe National Oatmeal Month than in January? Ask family members to name a variety of toppings they'd like to have on oatmeal, such as raisins or blueberries. Then fix oatmeal for breakfast one morning and set out each requested topping in a separate bowl. Invite each family member to add a topping or two to a bowl of oatmeal and enjoy a nutritious breakfast. Mmmm! That's a warm and delicious way to start the morning!

Hat Day

You don't need a hat to celebrate Hat Day (the third Friday in January), just a bit of creativity! Have each family member draw a self-portrait on a sheet of paper. Be sure each person leaves room at the top to add a hat later. Ask family members to trade pictures with one another. (Or if you prefer, use a photocopier to enlarge a photograph of each family member. Give each family member a photocopy of another person.) Have each person use fabric scraps, construction paper, markers, scissors, and glue to create a snazzy hat on the picture. Then ask each family member to cut it out, keeping the person and hat in one piece. Allow the picture to dry overnight. Then display the finished artwork on the refrigerator or in the family photo album.

Note To The Teacher: Give one copy of this reproducible to each student at the beginning of the month. Encourage each family to complete at least one activity by the end of January.

HOORAY FOR THE NEW YEAR!

Who says the festivities have to end? Usher in the new year with these seasonal activities and let the celebrations continue!

Ending It Right

Youngsters will get a handle on suffixes with this "ap-peal-ing" bell activity! Give each child a copy of page 6. Instruct him to complete the page by following the directions at the top of the page. Then give each child a construction-paper copy of page 7, a jingle bell, and a paper clip. To complete the project, each student cuts out the construction-paper bells. Then he carefully slides the jingle bell onto the paper clip as shown. He glues the paper clip onto the back of one of the paper bells so that the jingle bell hangs below the cutout. Then he glues the backs of the bells together, sandwiching the paper clip in between. Next he cuts apart each sentence on page 6 and glues it to the appropriate side of the bell. Display students' work as a border around a New Year's bulletin board, such as the one suggested in "Sands Through The Hourglass" on this page. Youngsters will give this idea a ringing endorsement!

Name Sarah Jones
Good-bye, 1999
I really liked summer vacation in 1999. My family and I visited my uncle Mike in Florida. We swam with the dolphins.
Hello, 2000
This summer I hope I can go visit my best friend in Atlanta. Annie moved away, and I miss her a lot!

Sands Through The Hourglass

Another year slips away, and a brand-new year begins—what a great writing opportunity! Give each student a copy of page 8. Instruct each student to fill in the appropriate years (see the illustration). At the top of the hourglass, have her write about a memorable event of last year. Then, at the bottom, have her write about what she would like to have happen in the upcoming year. Have her color and cut out the hourglass and, if desired, glue sand (or glitter, if sand is not available) to the pattern without covering the writing. Display the finished work on a bulletin board trimmed with the bells from "Ending It Right" on this page. What a timely way to ring in the new year!

Name____

Ring In The New Year

Read each sentence.
Fill in the blank with the ending *-d, -ed,* or *-ing.*

1. My family was want_____ to do something special for New Year's Eve.	6. People were laugh_____ and sing_____.
2. We decide_____ to have a party!	7. At midnight, the car horns began sound_____ very loud.
3. We ask_____ all our friends to come.	8. The dogs were bark_____ from all the noise!
4. They all arrived wear_____ party clothes.	9. Then we all yell_____, "Happy New Year!"
5. My friend Max play_____ his horn at the party.	10. The year end_____ with a bang!

Note To The Teacher: Use with "Ending It Right" on page 5.

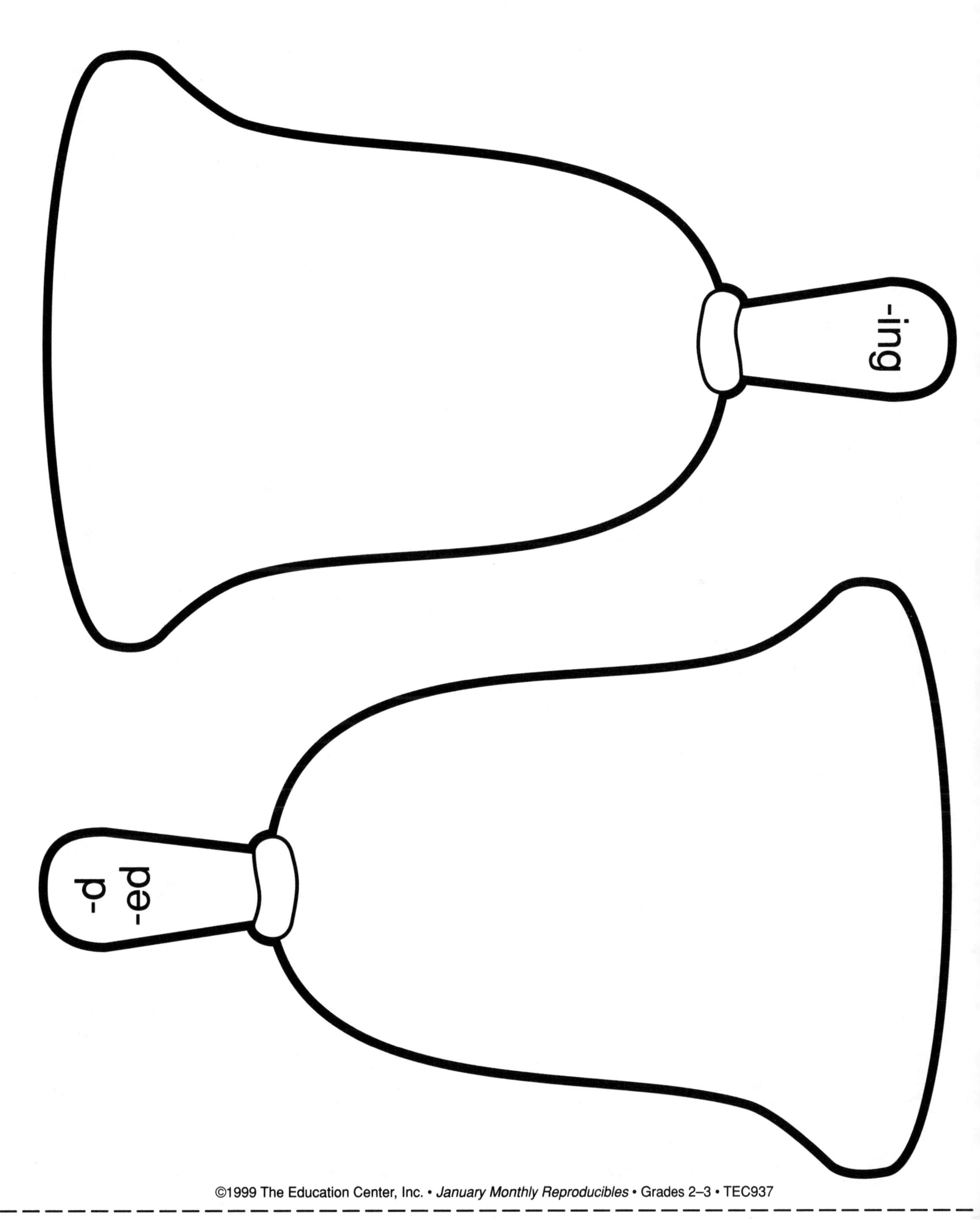

Note To The Teacher: Use with “Ending It Right” on page 5.

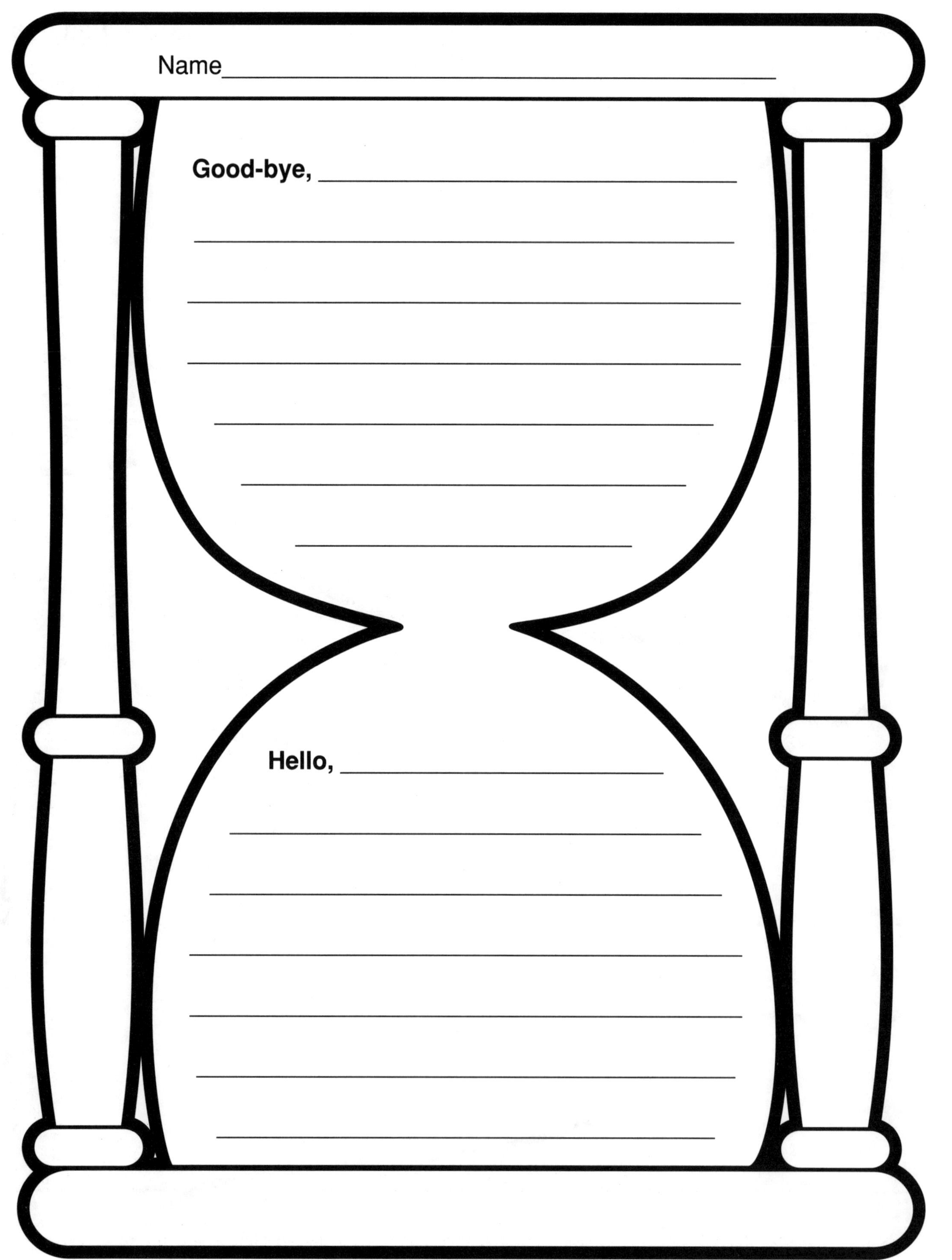

Note To The Teacher: Use with "Sands Through The Hourglass" on page 5.

Name ______________________________

Party Time

Get ready for a New Year's Eve party!
Color the coins needed to buy each item.

Bonus Box: For each party item, show the amount of change needed if it had been bought with a dollar bill. Show your work on the back of this paper.

 Name ____________________

A Message With Value

What's the secret message?
Cut out the place values at the bottom of the page.
Glue each place value to its matching balloon.
Then read the message.

e 9 tens	**a** 6 hundreds	**H** 9 ones	**o** 4 hundreds	**e** 0 tens	**a** 5 tens	**l** 6 ones	**w** 7 ones
r! 2 tens	**a** 4 tens	**c** 7 tens	**n** 3 tens	**v** 8 ones	**y** 0 ones	**e** 6 tens	**o** 5 hundreds

HONORING MARTIN LUTHER KING, JR.

Civil rights leader Martin Luther King, Jr., was born on January 15, 1929, in Atlanta, Georgia. His birthday is a federal holiday and is celebrated the third Monday of January. Teach students about Dr. King *and* reinforce skills with these memorable activities.

Martin Luther King, Jr., Timeline

Motivate students to apply both their inference and sequencing skills as they learn more about Dr. King. Give each student a copy of page 12 and a yarn length approximately 22 inches long. Ask student volunteers to read aloud the information about Dr. King. Then instruct each student to cut out the boxes on the bold lines, color each picture, and glue each illustration to its appropriate text box. Next have her determine which box tells about the event that occurred first, then fold its edge on the indicated line. Instruct her to slide the yarn under the resulting flap, position it so it is first (see the illustration), and glue the flap closed. Have her continue in this manner until the six events are suspended from the yarn in sequential order. Display the timelines on a bulletin board titled "The Times Of Dr. King."

Martin Luther King, Jr., was born in Atlanta, Georgia, in 1929.

King married Coretta Scott in 1953.

Books To Dream By

Weave these inspiring books into your study of Dr. King, and students will discover that there are many powerful ways to envision the future.

Mammoth Magic by Shelley Gill (Paws IV Publishing, 1986)

Africa Dream by Eloise Greenfield (HarperCollins Children's Books, 1992)

Beardream by Will Hobbs (Atheneum Books For Young Readers, 1997)

Appelemando's Dreams by Patricia Polacco (Paperstar, 1997)

The Sign Painter's Dream by Roger Roth (Crown Publishers, Inc.; 1993)

Hopes And Dreams

Dr. King was a man filled with aspirations for all people. He peacefully worked for equal and fair treatment of Black Americans. He dreamed of a day when people would not be judged by the color of their skin. Share this information with students; then encourage them to talk about their own hopes and dreams. Next give each child a copy of page 13. Instruct her to write about and illustrate a dream she has for herself, her family, her school, and her neighborhood. Then provide time for students to share their responses with one another.

fold

King married Coretta Scott in 1953.

fold

In 1954 King became a preacher at a church in Montgomery, Alabama.

fold

Martin Luther King, Jr., was born in Atlanta, Georgia, in 1929.

fold

King was shot and killed in 1968.

fold

King gave his “I Have A Dream” speech on August 28, 1963.

fold

King was awarded the Nobel prize for peace in 1964.

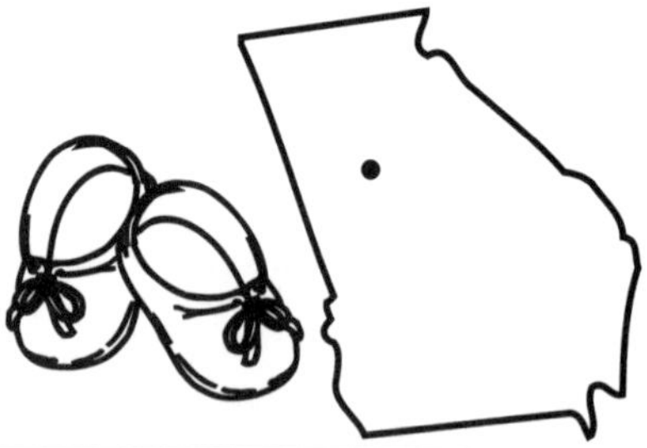

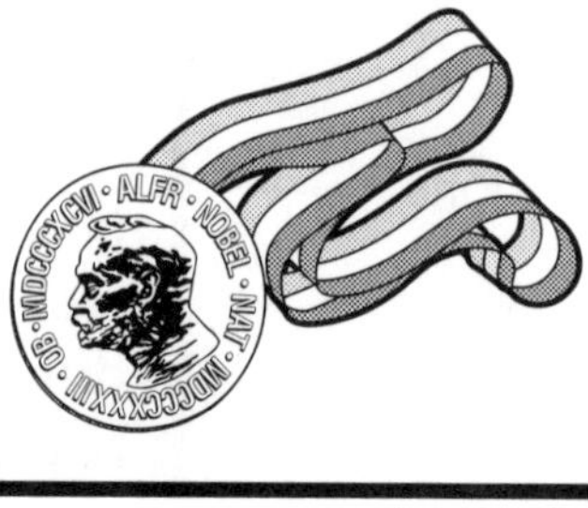

Note To The Teacher: Use with “Martin Luther King, Jr. Timeline” on page 11.

Name

Note To The Teacher: Use with "Hopes And Dreams" on page 11.

Name ______________________________

Fact Or Opinion?

Cut out each picture.
Read each statement below.
If the statement is a fact, glue a picture of Dr. King beside it.
If the statement is an opinion, glue a picture of the child beside it.

1. Dr. King was a good speaker.
2. Dr. King gave speeches all around the United States.
3. The Nobel prize for peace was awarded to Dr. King.
4. The most important award to be given is the Nobel prize.
5. Dr. King was the best preacher Alabama ever had.
6. Dr. King preached in Alabama.
7. Dr. King gave his "I Have A Dream" speech in Washington, DC.
8. "I Have A Dream" was Dr. King's best speech.
9. Dr. King's birthday is a federal holiday.
10. It would be fun to have a birthday party on Dr. King's birthday.

BILL PEET
A Storytime Treat

January celebrations are not complete until "Happy Birthday" is sung to Bill Peet! Celebrate the January 29 birthday of this beloved author/illustrator by introducing your youngsters to the whimsical animal characters that fill his books. From a worldly pig who wants to join the circus to a kindhearted zebra who adopts an ostrich chick, Peet's characters will turn the coldest January day into a heartwarming celebration!

Kindness In Deed

Can a zebra help teach kindness? If she's one of Bill Peet's characters, she can! Reinforce the concept of good deeds with *Zella, Zack, & Zodiac* (Houghton Mifflin Company, 1989). In this story, a benevolent zebra helps a young ostrich in need. When the zebra needs help, she finds her act of charity returned. Read this book aloud to students and talk about acts of kindness. Then cut slips of paper and program each with a different student's name. Give each student a copy of page 16 and have him randomly select a slip. Instruct him to complete and color the reproducible about the classmate named on his slip of paper. Display the completed pages on a bulletin board titled "Kindness Counts!"

Rolling Review

Keep students thinking about key elements of a story with this review activity! Give each student a copy of page 17. Have the student color, cut out, and assemble her two wheels with a brad (see the illustration). Then read aloud one of Bill Peet's books (refer to the list below). Have a student roll a die and announce the resulting number. Direct students to turn their wheels to that number. Then ask a volunteer to respond to the prompt that is showing on the wheel. Repeat the activity until several of the prompts on the wheel have been discussed. When it comes to recalling details, students will be on a roll!

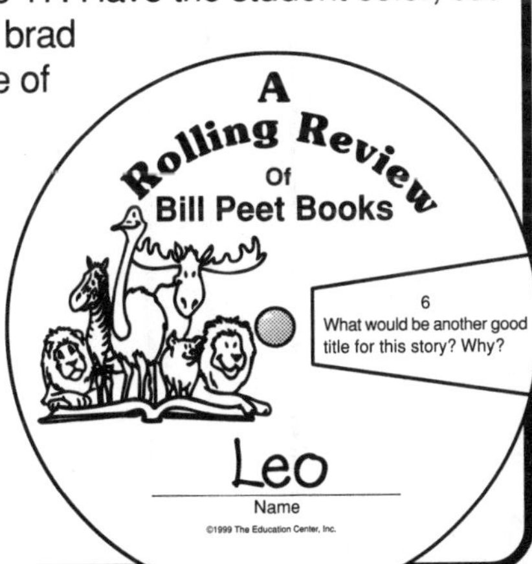

How Sweet Peet Is!

Share a few of these Bill Peet treats with students!

Cowardly Clyde (Houghton Mifflin Company, 1984)
Eli (Houghton Mifflin Company, 1984)
The Gnats Of Knotty Pine (Houghton Mifflin Company, 1984)
Hubert's Hair-Raising Adventure (Houghton Mifflin Company, 1979)
Kermit The Hermit (Houghton Mifflin Company, 1980)
The Wump World (Houghton Mifflin Company, 1991)

Name ____

Kindness Counts!

I would like to tell you about ______________________________.
Classmate's Name

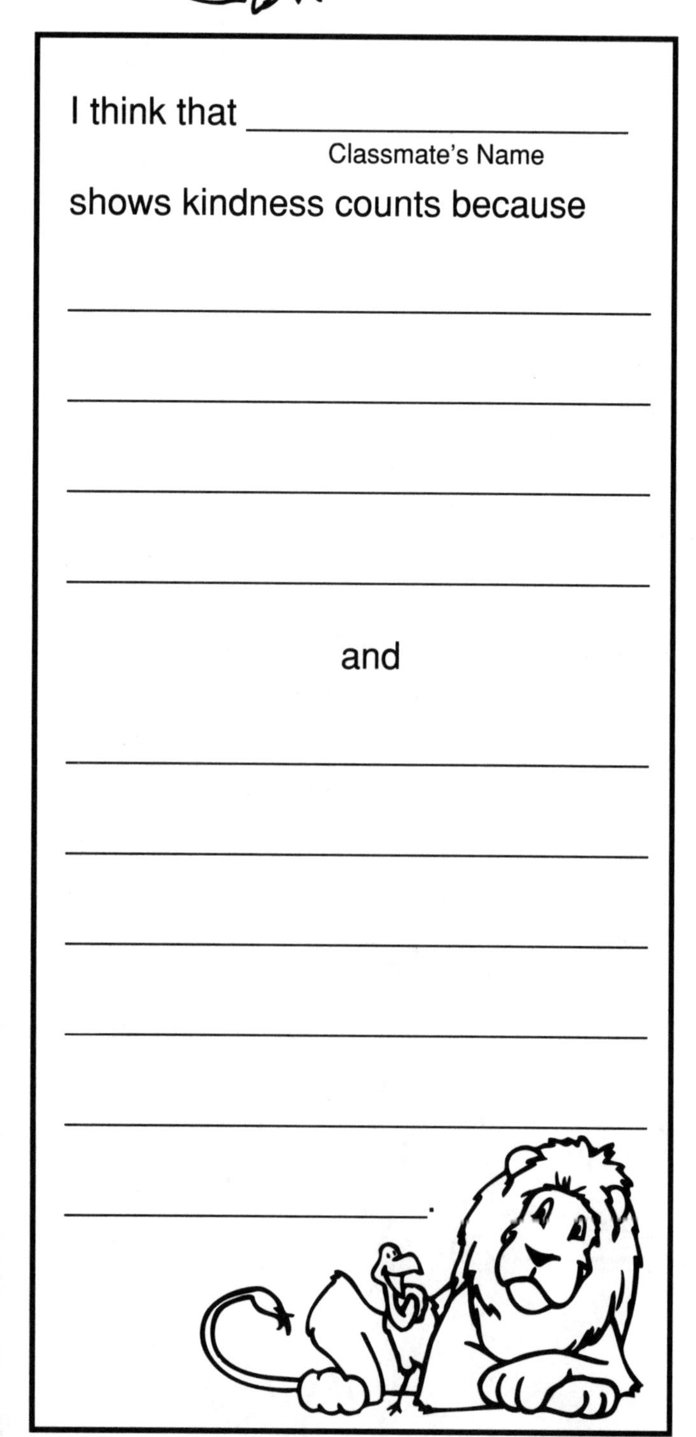

I think that ______________________
Classmate's Name
shows kindness counts because

____

____

____

____

and

____

____

____

____

____

______________________.

Here is a picture of

____
Classmate's Name

showing that kindness counts.

 Note To The Teacher: Use with "Kindness In Deed" on page 15.

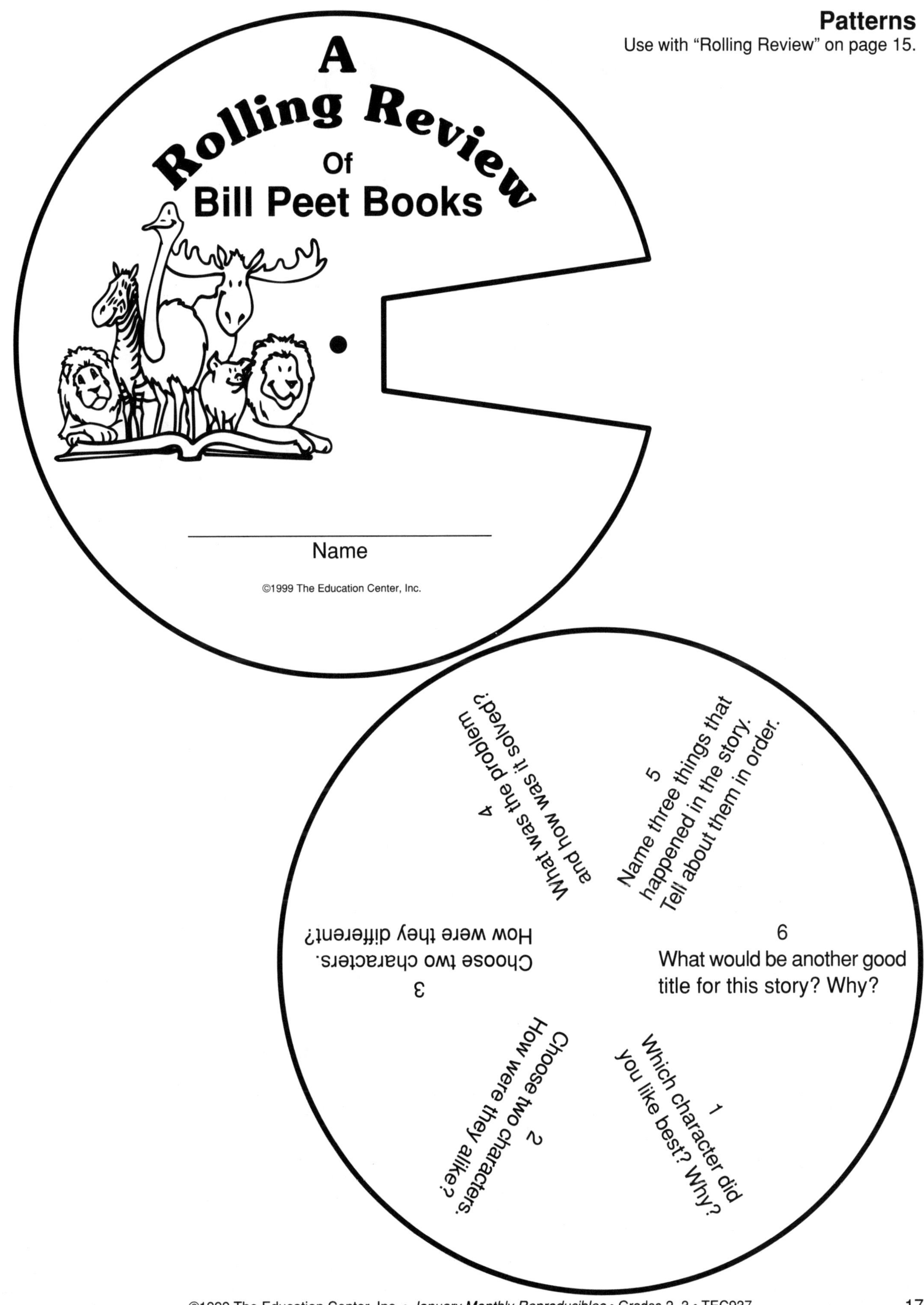
A
Rolling Review
Of
Bill Peet Books
Name
©1999 The Education Center, Inc.
1
Which character did you like best? Why?
2
Choose two characters.
How were they alike?
3
Choose two characters.
How were they different?
4
What was the problem
and how was it solved?
5
Name three things that
happened in the story.
Tell about them in order.
6
What would be another good
title for this story? Why?

Name____

Farmyard Facts And Opinions

Read each sentence.
Color the facts **pink.**
Color the opinions **yellow.**

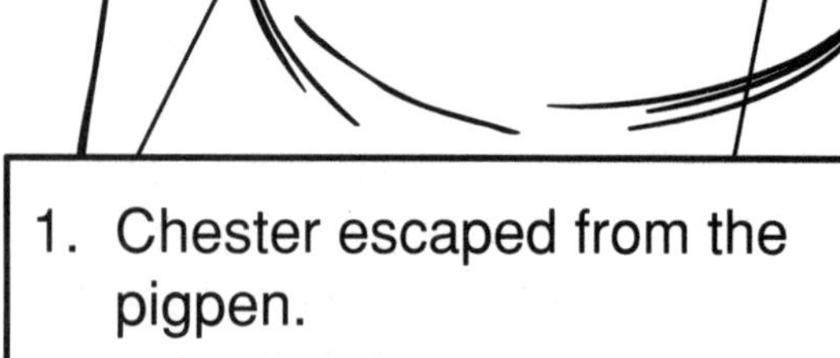

1. Chester escaped from the pigpen.
2. It would be fun to join the circus.
3. Chester was put in a cage with tigers.
4. Roscoe pushed the pig in a baby carriage.
5. Tigers are beautiful animals.

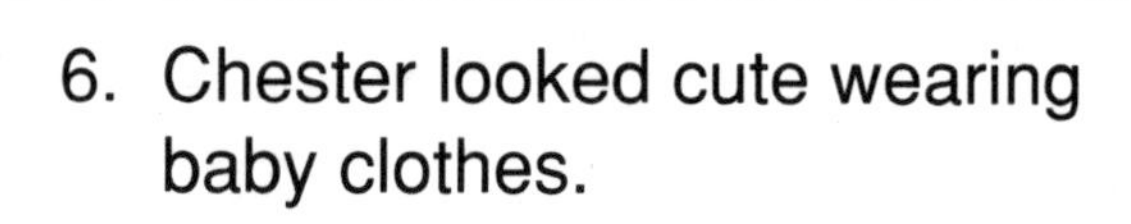

6. Chester looked cute wearing baby clothes.
7. Clowns are the best part of the circus.
8. Chester went back to the country.
9. Chester ate and ate until he was huge.
10. Chester was a very handsome pig.

 Note To The Teacher: Use with *Chester The Worldly Pig* by Bill Peet (Houghton Mifflin Company, 1980).

"Brrr-ing" On The Polar Animals!

Animals of the icy Arctic Circle and the nearly barren Antarctic serve as inspiration for these cool activities that will make students shiver with excitement!

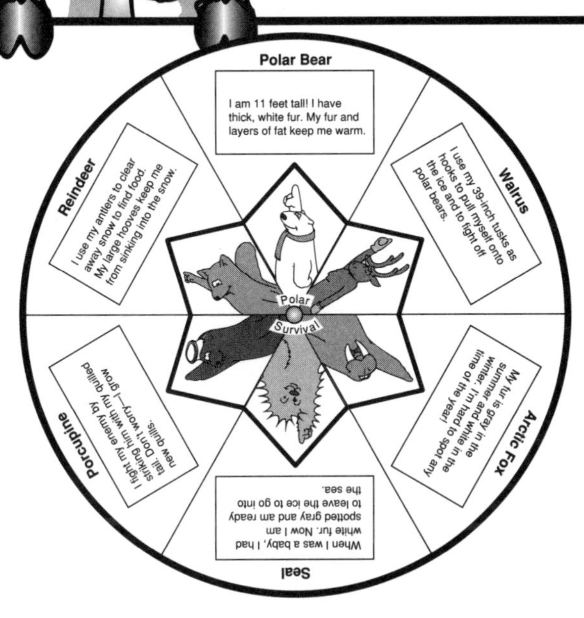

Survival Matchup

How do polar animals thrive in their harsh environment? Use this information-packed activity to send students spinning for the answers! Give each child a copy of page 20 and a brad. Have a volunteer read aloud one of the passages in the lower right-hand corner. Encourage discussion about the animal and its special ability to survive. Repeat this step until each passage has been read and discussed. Next instruct each student to cut out the pattern pieces, reread each passage, and glue it below the appropriate animal's name. Have her color the animals and attach them to the center of the circle with a brad. Allow time for students to review the information by working in pairs. Instruct students in each pair to take turns choosing an animal, moving that animal to point to its description on the wheel, and reading the information aloud. Youngsters will be amazed—the keys to survival for polar animals are fascinating!

Guide Words On Ice

Invite youngsters to practice their dictionary skills with the help of these polar pals! To make this engaging center, duplicate four copies of page 21 on tagboard. Color, cut out, and, if desired, laminate the animals and icebergs. Next staple each iceberg along the bottom and sides to the front of a letter-sized envelope to form a pocket as shown. Repeat this step for the remaining three envelopes. Then write a polar-related word, such as those shown below, on each animal. Program each iceberg with a different pair of guide words so that each polar-related word comes between one of the four sets of guide words. Then store the animals in a string-tie envelope. To make the activity self-checking, write the correct answers on an index card and store it in the appropriate envelope.

To use the center, the student chooses a polar pal from the envelope and decides between which set of guide words it belongs. Then she places it in the appropriate iceberg pocket. When all animals have been placed, she checks her answers. This icy activity will be as easy as ABC!

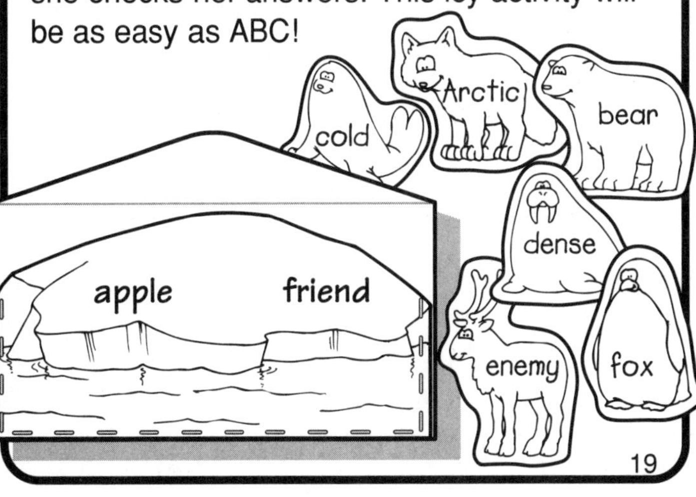

Patterns

Use with "Survival Matchup" on page 19.

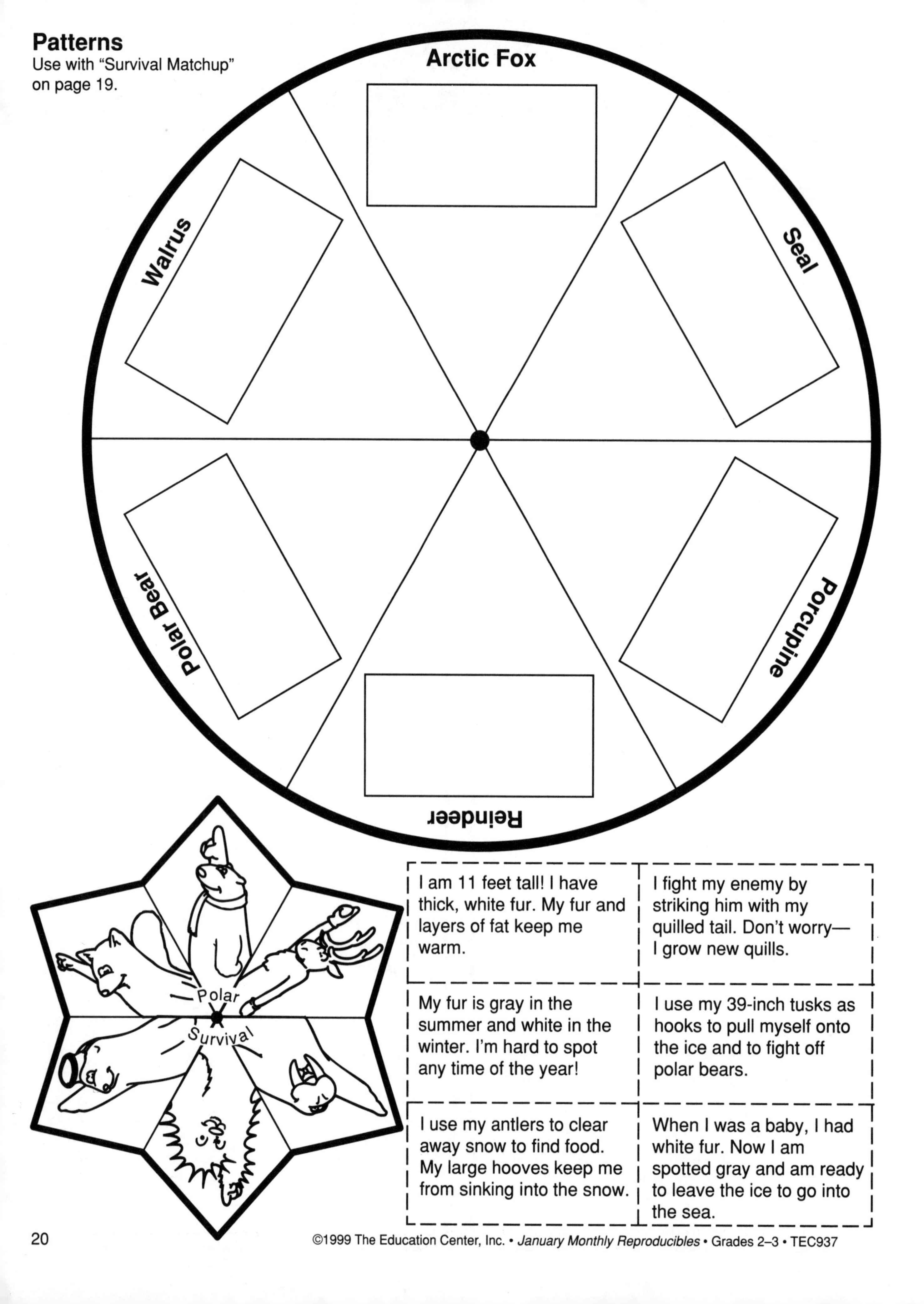

I am 11 feet tall! I have thick, white fur. My fur and layers of fat keep me warm.	I fight my enemy by striking him with my quilled tail. Don't worry—I grow new quills.
My fur is gray in the summer and white in the winter. I'm hard to spot any time of the year!	I use my 39-inch tusks as hooks to pull myself onto the ice and to fight off polar bears.
I use my antlers to clear away snow to find food. My large hooves keep me from sinking into the snow.	When I was a baby, I had white fur. Now I am spotted gray and am ready to leave the ice to go into the sea.

Patterns

Use with "Guide Words On Ice" on page 19.

Name ______________________________

Where Am I?

The Arctic is located at the top of the world. Many animals make their homes in different regions of the Arctic.

At the center of the Arctic is an ice-covered sea or **polar sea.**

Surrounding the ice-covered sea is a desert called a **tundra.** It is flat and treeless. Strong winds blow away the little snow that falls. It can be very rocky.

South of the tundra is a **taiga** (TY guh). It has large, evergreen forests. Snow can be deep in the taiga.

Read about the Arctic animals.
Decide if the animal is living in a *polar sea,* a *tundra,* or a *taiga.* Write the answer on the line.

 **Seal** I am feeding on small sea animals. 1. ____________	 **Siberian Tiger** I am slinking through the woods. My stripes are my camouflage.  2. ____________	 **Lynx** My kittens are living in a hollow log. When they grow up, they will need to use their large paws like snowshoes.  3. ____________	 **Falcon** I am getting ready to lay my eggs on a rocky ledge. Sometimes I will lay them on open ground. 4. ____________
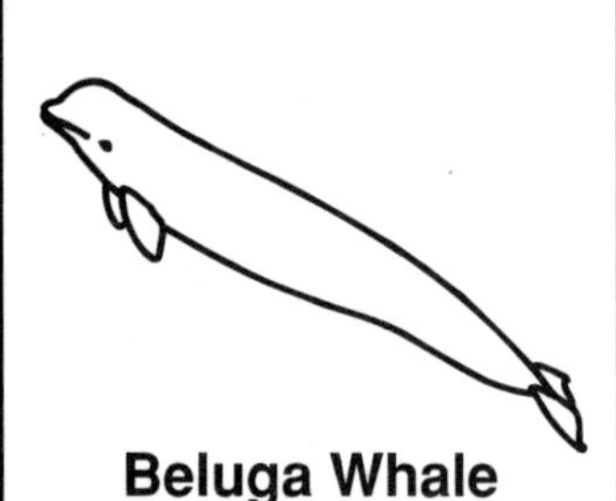 **Beluga Whale** I am making echoing sounds so that I will not bump into icebergs. 5. ____________	 **Reindeer** I am making a journey across treeless land. It is the longest migration made by any land animal. 6. ____________	 **Polar Bear** I am watching seals rest on the ice. I will surprise them by swimming up and pouncing on them. 7. ____________	 **Wolf** My pack and I are hunting reindeer. 8. ____________

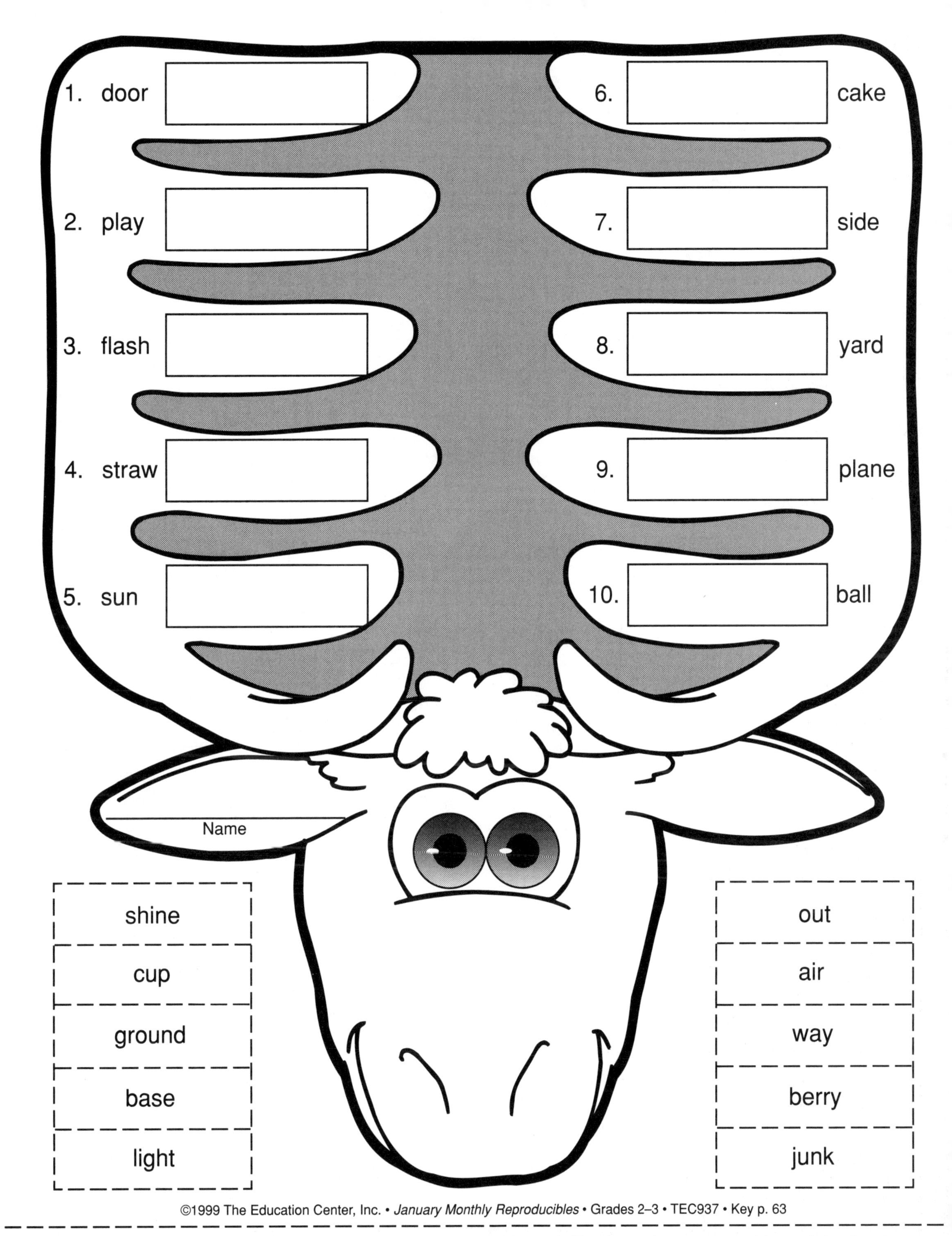

Note To The Teacher: Give each student a copy of this page. Have her read the words. Then instruct her to cut out each box and place it next to one of the antler words to form a compound word. When all words have been arranged, have her glue the words into place and cut out the reindeer. Display the reindeer on a bulletin board titled "Antler Antics!"

Name ______________________________

Feeding On The Facts

Solve each problem.
Cross out the matching answer in the fish.
Hint: There are three extra fish.

1. 145 + 236	2. 252 + 471	3. 631 + 229	4. 427 + 392	5. 668 + 123
6. 444 + 261	7. 378 + 312	8. 821 + 129	9. 117 + 336	10. 432 + 193
11. 247 + 118	12. 581 + 297	13. 221 + 696	14. 670 + 159	15. 103 + 118

Positively Penguins

Growing weary of winter? Perk up with these sure-to-please penguin activities! Practicing math and reading skills has never been so cool!

Birds Of A Feather

Penguins are easily recognized by their black and white "attire." Help youngsters discover other distinctive penguin features *and* learn about another famous feathered friend with this unique Venn diagram! Give each student a copy of page 26. Ask students to read aloud and discuss the information about penguins and robins. To complete the activity, each student colors and cuts out the birds and their signs. Then he cuts out each box containing a bird fact, reads it, and glues it to the appropriate bird or to the egg. He glues each sign to a craft stick. Then he glues each stick to the appropriate wing along the fold line. He folds over and glues down each wing tip. Then he takes his project home and reads it to a family member or friend.

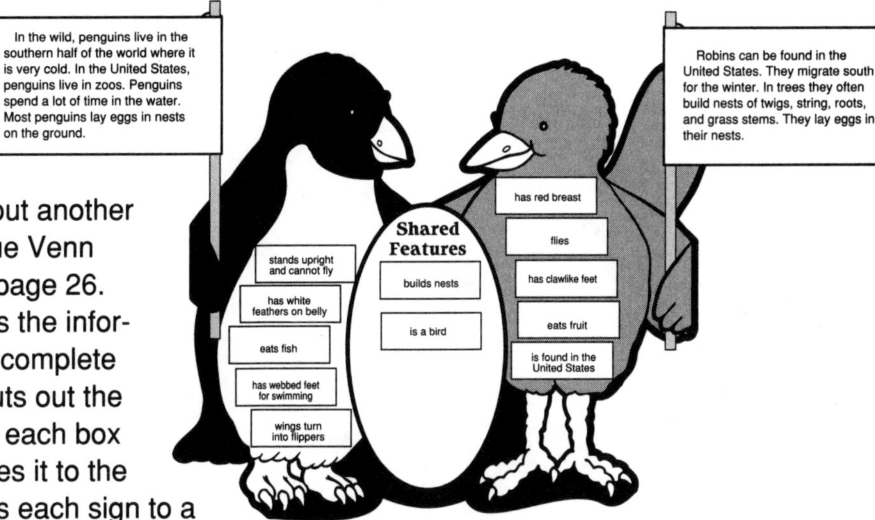

Penguin Pendants

Dressing for chilly weather just got more stylish with these appealing penguin pendants! Have each youngster follow these directions to make a pendant. Invite all your youngsters to don their projects and parade them proudly.

Materials for each student:
plastic spoon
prepared plaster of paris mix
petroleum jelly
paper clip
two small wiggle eyes
black and orange tempera paint
small paintbrushes
length of yarn
glue

Directions:
1. Apply a thin coat of petroleum jelly to the bowl of the spoon.
2. Fill the spoon with plaster of paris mix and level off so the top is smooth.
3. Place a paper clip on top of the mix so that a loop is formed as shown.
4. Allow to set overnight.
5. Remove the pendant from the spoon.
6. Using the pointed end as the head, paint the rounded side to look like a penguin.
7. Glue on wiggle eyes.
8. Thread a length of yarn through the loop and tie the ends together.

"Eggs-traordinary" Emperors

When it comes to birds, we usually think of nests. But for the emperor penguin, who lives in a barren land, a nest is not easily built! Explain to students that a female emperor penguin lays her egg on the ground and then returns to the sea. To keep the egg warm, the male emperor rolls it on top of his feet and tucks it under his warm belly. The males huddle together until the eggs hatch about two months later. Mom penguin returns to care for the chick, and Dad looks for food.

After sharing these facts, encourage discussion about the consequences of an emperor dad moving around with an egg tucked under his belly. Then challenge students to an emperor shuffle! Have each student carefully balance a beanbag on top of her feet, encouraging her to shuffle around the room as she keeps the beanbag in place. After all students have tried the shuffle, give each a copy of page 27. Instruct her to write about the experience through the eyes of an emperor dad. This activity is sure to melt away those winter humdrums!

In the wild, penguins live in the southern half of the world where it is very cold. In the United States, penguins live in zoos. Penguins spend a lot of time in the water. Most penguins lay eggs in nests on the ground.

Robins can be found in the United States. They migrate south for the winter. In trees they often build nests of twigs, string, roots, and grass stems. They lay eggs in their nests.

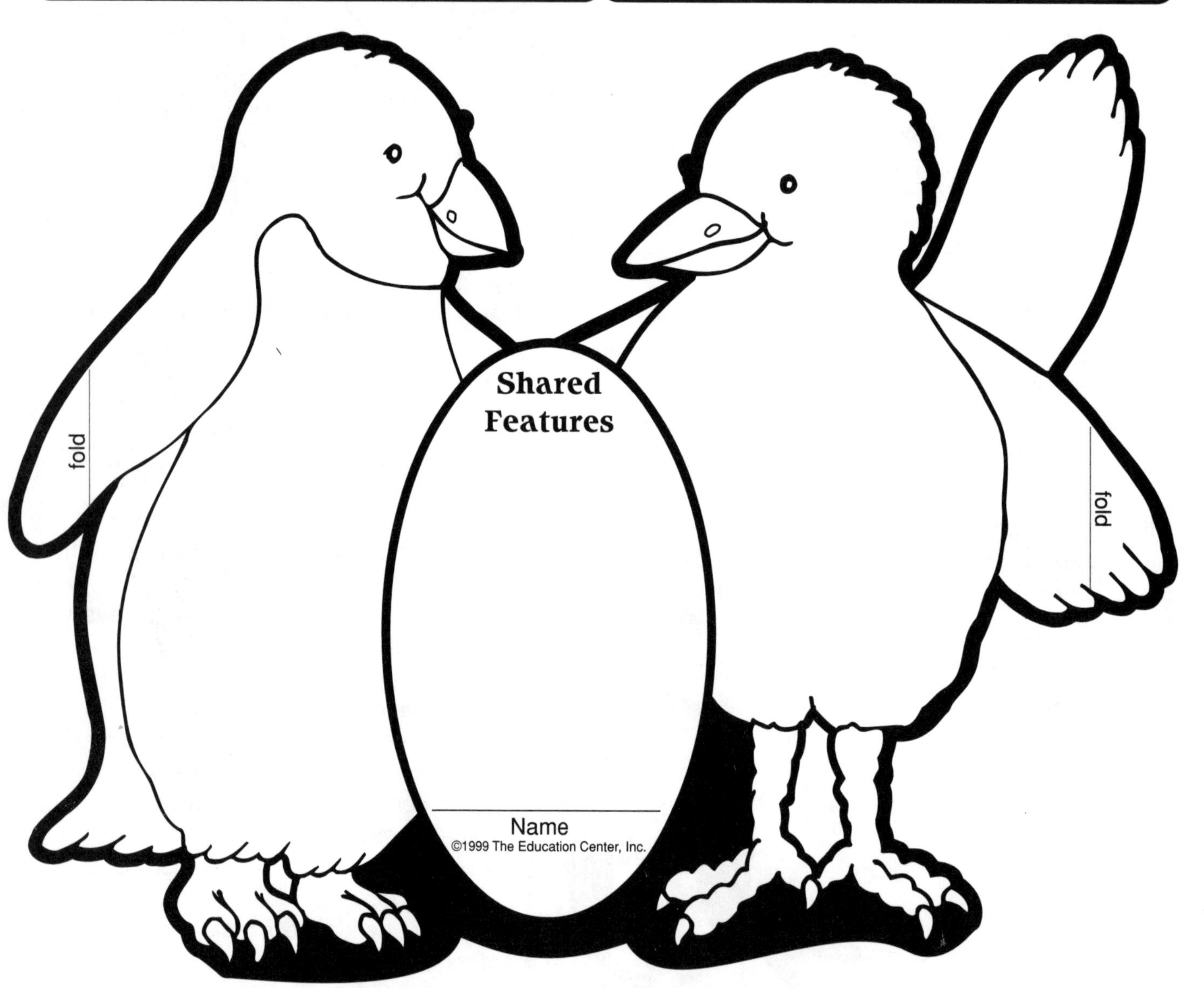

is found in the United States	wings turn into flippers	flies
has red breast	is a bird	has white feathers on belly
has webbed feet for swimming	eats fish	stands upright and cannot fly
builds nests	eats fruit	has clawlike feet

 Note To The Teacher: Use with “Birds Of A Feather” on page 25.

Note To The Teacher: Use with " 'Eggs-traordinary' Emperors" on page 25.

Name ______________________________

Arctic ABC Order

Brrr! It's cold!
Warm up by putting these wintry words in ABC order.

cold
chilly
white
winter
beak
bird
black
waddle

1. ______________________
2. ______________________
3. ______________________
4. ______________________
5. ______________________
6. ______________________
7. ______________________
8. ______________________

ice
wing
flippers
water
feathers
fish
swimmer
igloo

1. ______________________
2. ______________________
3. ______________________
4. ______________________
5. ______________________
6. ______________________
7. ______________________
8. ______________________

Bonus Box: Choose five words from the lists. On the back of this paper, write a sentence using each one.

Name ____________________

Penguin Party

Read each problem.
Cross out the number you don't need to answer the question.
Then solve the problem.

1. Petey Penguin is planning a party.
   He bought 12 red balloons, 7 green balloons, and 20 party hats.
   How many balloons did he buy in all?

2. Peggy is helping Petey with the food.
   She made 2 cakes and 14 jelly sandwiches. She ate 3 of the sandwiches.
   How many sandwiches does she have left?

3. Petey invited 20 penguins to the party.
   Six penguins will be out of town and 2 will be coming in a new car.
   How many of the penguins invited will be at the party?

4. Petey wants to have prizes for the party games.
   He bought 9 blue ribbons, 8 gold medals, and 2 boxes to put them in.
   How many prizes did he buy altogether?

5. Peggy's camera has 18 pictures left on the film.
   Last year she took 10 pictures at the party. She will take 12 pictures tonight.
   How many pictures will she have left?

6. Pam is going to sing at the party.
   She has learned 13 fast songs, 5 slow songs, and 11 new dance steps.
   How many songs has she learned?

7. Pam helped Petey set up for the party.
   They moved 3 tables, 6 benches, and 8 chairs.
   How many things are there for them to sit on?

8. Peggy and Pam will give each guest something to wear.
   There are 9 blue hats, 6 fancy headbands, and 7 yellow hats.
   How many hats are there?

Bonus Box: On the back of this paper, write a word problem that has extra information. Ask a friend to solve the problem.

Name______________________________

Something's Fishy!

Read each sentence.
Write the correct word in each blank.

Remember—*homophones* are words that sound alike but have different spellings and meanings!

knew
new

ate
eight

way
weigh

whole
hole

one
won

see
sea

1. The penguin ____________ a lot of fish for dinner.
2. He had ______________ of them in all!
3. He ate the _______________ batch!
4. He fished for them through a __________ in the ice.
5. He ____________ he had a fish when he felt a tug on his line.
6. When the line breaks, he uses a ______________ one.
7. He catches many fish that ________________.
8. Some of them _________________ over ten pounds!
9. The penguin _________________ a fishing contest.
10. The fish he caught was the biggest ____________.
11. Did you _____________ the fish he caught yesterday?
12. It's fun to find food in the _____________!

Bonus Box: On the back of the paper, write the homophone(s) of these words: *to, buy, bee, sew.*

INCREDIBLE INVENTORS

Celebrate inventor Benjamin Franklin's January birthdate with this high-flying inventors unit. No doubt students' learning will reach new heights!

The Sky's The Limit!

Launch your inventors unit with this booklet idea and teach students what all great inventors know—the sky's the limit with creative problem solving. Give each student a copy of pages 32, 33, and 34. Have her read and complete the booklet pages as directed. Ask each youngster to personalize and color her cover, and then cut out her cover and pages along the bold lines. Next instruct her to sequence the pages and staple them together with the cover as shown. After having each student share her completed booklet with classmates, encourage her to read it to a family member at home.

Pretzels

(Makes approximately 24 pretzels)

Ingredients:

- 3 cups warm water
- 2 envelopes yeast
- 9–10 cups flour
- 2 teaspoons salt
- 2 tablespoons sugar
- 2 eggs
- coarse salt

Mix the water, yeast, and sugar in a small bowl. Let the mixture stand for five minutes. Combine the salt and 9 cups of flour in a large bowl. Then add the yeast mixture. Stir. If the dough is sticky, gradually add more flour.

Lightly flour hands and form the dough into shapes. Place the shapes on a tray lined with parchment paper. Beat the eggs in a small bowl and brush them onto the dough. Sprinkle the dough with coarse salt. Bake at 425° for 12 minutes or until lightly browned.

Tasty Inventions

What happens when a duke challenges a baker to invent a new roll? A tasty new treat is created! Help students re-create the baker's ingenious solution with this literature-based activity. Prepare a class supply of pretzel dough using the recipe shown. Then, taking care not to reveal the back cover, read aloud part of *Walter The Baker* by Eric Carle (Simon & Schuster Books For Young Readers, 1995). Interrupt the reading right after the Duke gives Walter the order to make a new kind of roll.

Next ask each student to try his hand at following the Duke's order to invent, with only one piece of dough, a roll through which the rising sun can shine three times. Give each youngster a portion of the prepared dough. Have him lightly flour his hands, then shape the dough on a sheet of waxed paper. When he is satisfied that his creation meets the Duke's requirements, ask him to place it on a baking sheet lined with parchment paper. Instruct him to lightly brush the beaten eggs onto his dough, then sprinkle coarse salt over the top. With a permanent marker, have the student write his name beside his dough on the parchment paper. While the dough is baking, finish reading the story aloud. As students enjoy their delicious snacks, invite them to compare their dough creations to Walter's pretzels. Yum!

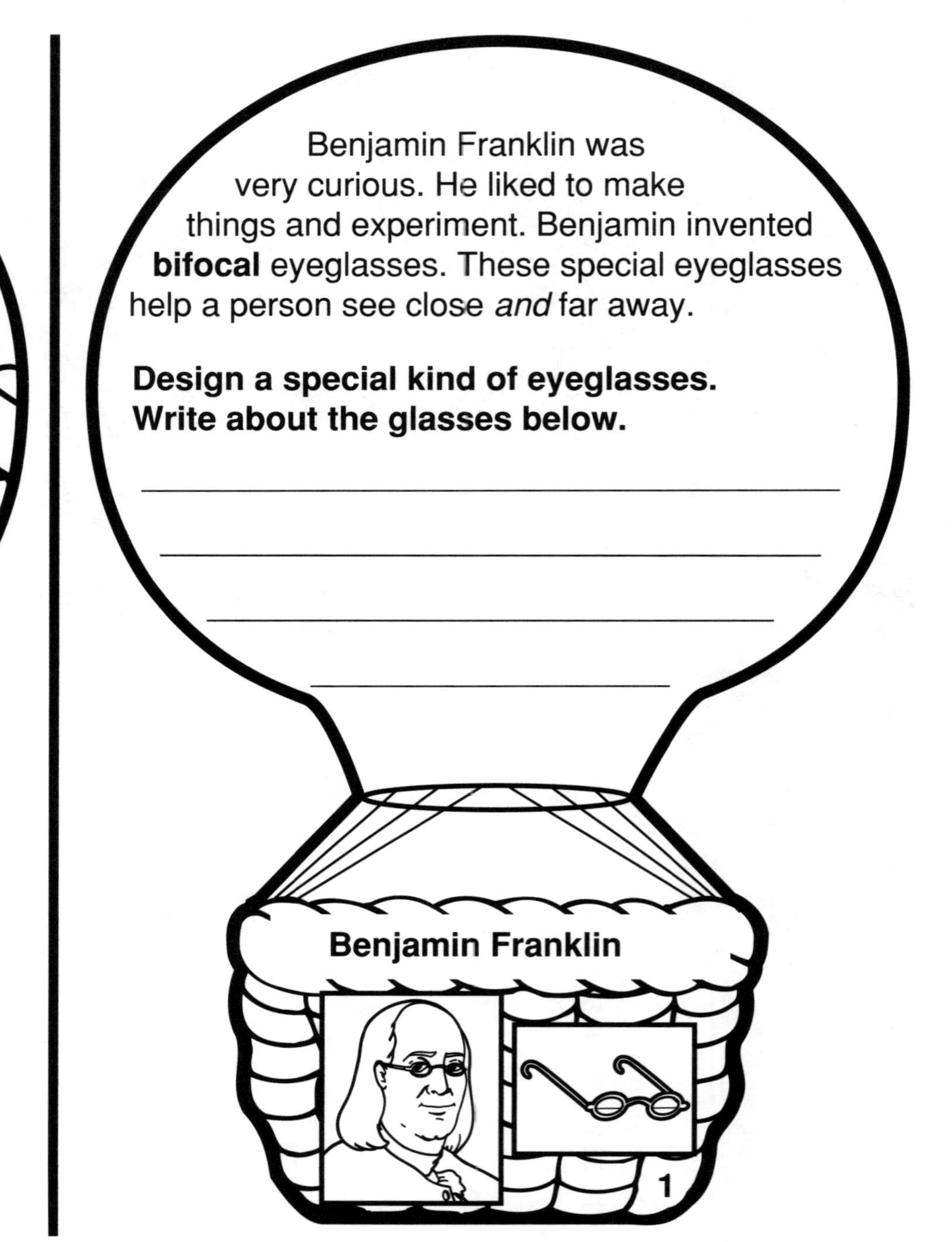

Benjamin Franklin was very curious. He liked to make things and experiment. Benjamin invented **bifocal** eyeglasses. These special eyeglasses help a person see close *and* far away.

Design a special kind of eyeglasses. Write about the glasses below.

____

____

____

____

Benjamin Franklin

1

 Note To The Teacher: Use with "The Sky's The Limit!" on page 31.

Note To The Teacher: Use with "The Sky's The Limit!" on page 31.

Marie Curie worked very hard in school and was an excellent student. She was the first woman to win a Nobel Prize. Marie helped discover **radium.** It is used to fight cancer.

Think of something you would like to learn more about.
Write a question about it below.

Marie Curie

RADIUM

4

George Washington Carver did many experiments with plants. He made ink, milk, and soap from peanuts. In fact, George invented more than 300 products from **peanuts!**

Invent a new way to use a carrot.
Write about it below.

 Note To The Teacher: Use with “The Sky’s The Limit!” on page 31.

Name ____________________

Up, Up, And Away!

Read about the invention of hot-air balloons.

Inventors Jacques and Joseph Montgolfier were brothers who lived in France. They liked to experiment. The brothers filled small paper bags with smoke. The bags rose in the air! At first the Montgolfiers thought the smoke caused the bags to rise. Later they found out that hot air made the bags rise. The brothers launched a smoke-filled balloon on June 4, 1783. The large cloth balloon was lined with paper. It was 35 feet in diameter. Jacques and Joseph were one of the first people to launch a hot-air balloon!

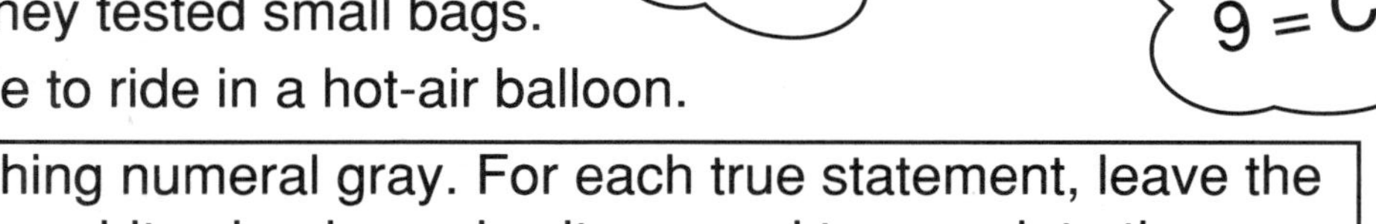

Read each statement carefully.
Circle T if it is true.
Circle F if it is false.

T F 1. The Montgolfiers lived in France.
T F 2. The brothers filled plastic bags with smoke.
T F 3. The Montgolfiers experimented with small paper bags.
T F 4. Smoke caused the small bags to rise.
T F 5. The brothers sent up a large balloon during the winter of 1783.
T F 6. The large balloon was filled with smoke.
T F 7. The brothers lined the cloth balloon with paper.
T F 8. After the Montgolfiers made the large balloon, they tested small bags.
T F 9. Jacques and Joseph were one of the first people to ride in a hot-air balloon.

For each false statement, color the cloud with the matching numeral gray. For each true statement, leave the matching cloud white. Then unscramble the letters in the white clouds, and write a word to complete the sentence below. A new invention starts with an ___ ___ ___ ___.

Name ____________________

Bright Idea

Solve each problem.

42 − 19 = S	64 − 38 = L	77 − 29 = A	75 − 46 = R	24 − 17 = N
82 − 33 = D	32 − 16 = K	56 − 9 = P	41 − 17 = W	61 − 24 = G
94 − 86 = O	87 − 8 = H	93 − 39 = I	37 − 9 = E	71 − 33 = T

Use the code to solve the riddle.
What did the alligator invent to decorate his bathroom wall?

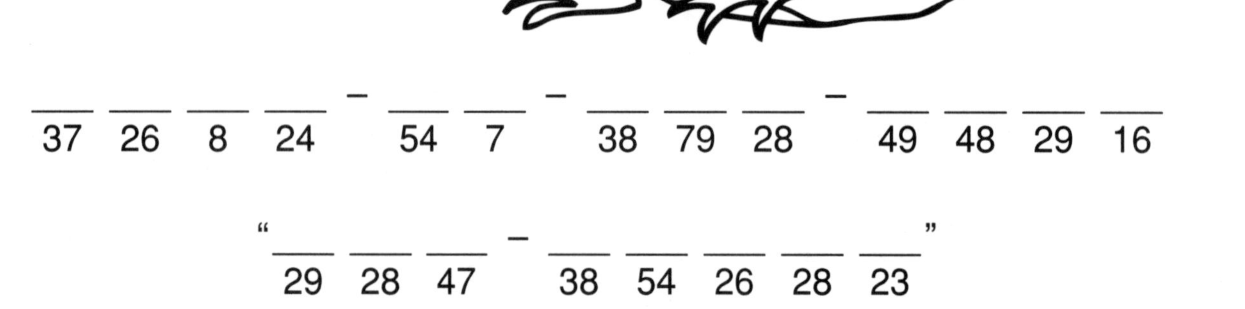

37 26 8 24 – 54 7 – 38 79 28 – 49 48 29 16

“29 28 47 – 38 54 26 28 23”

Bonus Box: On the back of this sheet, write a two-digit subtraction problem that has a difference of 5.

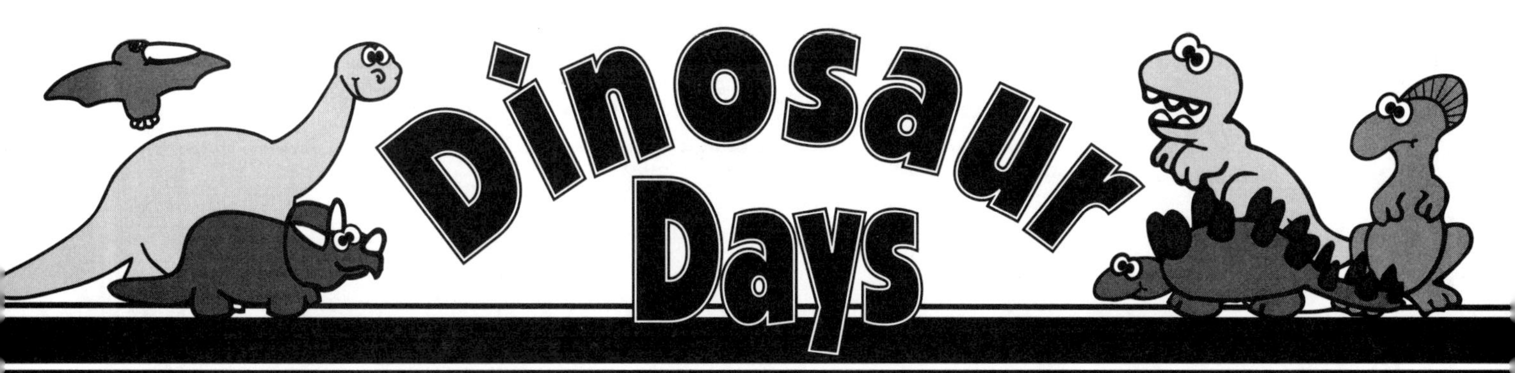

Brontosaurus, stegosaurus, tyrannosaurus...the gang's all here! Use these delightful dinosaur activities to make a *big* impression on your young paleontologists!

Dinosaur Dictionary

Dig into your study of dinosaurs with a "dino-mite" student-made dictionary! Share with students *An Alphabet Of Dinosaurs* by Peter Dodson (Scholastic Inc., 1995), *Be A Dinosaur Detective* by Dougal Dixon (Lerner Publications Company, 1988), or other nonfiction books about dinosaurs. Then assign each student a letter of the alphabet (some students may have more than one letter). Give each student a copy of page 38. Instruct him to complete the page by writing his assigned letter in the box and adding special terms, definitions, and illustrations that begin with that letter to the page. Next stack the papers in alphabetical order, staple them between two sheets of construction paper, and title the book "Dinosaur Dictionary." What a handy resource for boning up on dinosaur facts!

Prehistoric Prose

Tickle even the most fossilized funny bone with alliterative dinosaur fairy tales! Read aloud *Dinorella: A Prehistoric Fairy Tale* by Pamela Duncan Edwards (Hyperion Books For Children, 1997). Students will enjoy the Cinderella story line (tailored for slightly larger characters) as well as the alliterative narration. Then ask students to name alliterative phrases from the book. Next have them brainstorm words that could be used in alliteration with dinosaur names, such as *brontosaurus, tyrannosaurus,* and *kentrosaurus.* List youngsters' responses on the chalkboard. Then instruct each child to refer to the list and write an alliterative dinosaur story based on a favorite fairy tale. Provide time for each student to share her completed story with the class.

Rip-Roaring Art

Here's a dinosaur activity your young artists will tear into—no scissors allowed! Obtain a length of bulletin-board paper large enough for a class-size mural and an assortment of colored construction paper. Have each student carefully tear a sheet of construction paper into a dinosaur shape. Encourage her to create features for her dinosaur by gluing on pieces of contrasting colored paper or by using fine, felt-tipped markers. After her dinosaur is complete, have her tear background shapes—such as trees, volcanoes, or ponds—from construction paper. Have each student glue her creations onto the bulletin-board paper. Exhibit the completed mural in the hallway for a "tear-ific" display.

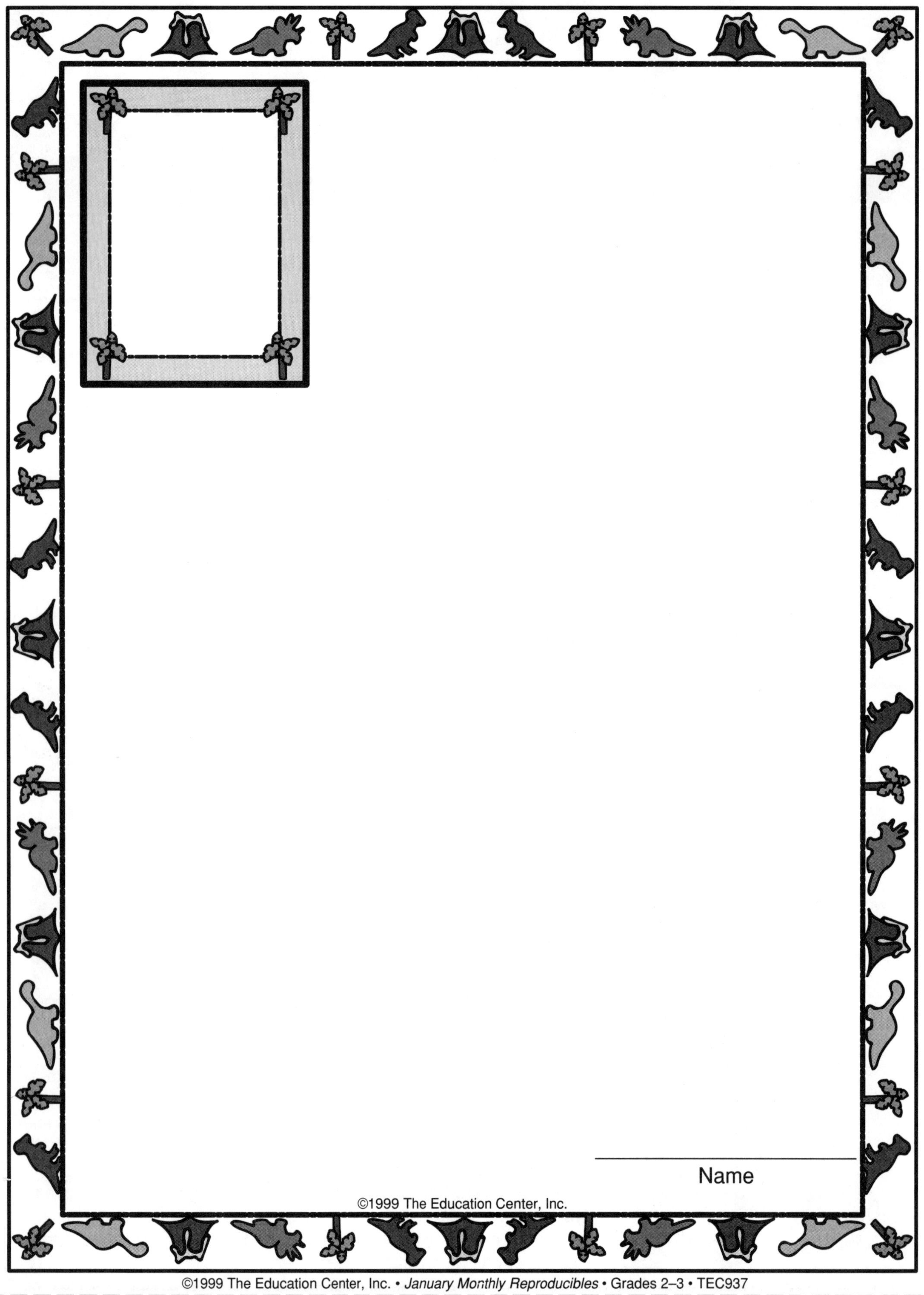

 Note To The Teacher: Use with "Dinosaur Dictionary" on page 37.

Note To The Teacher: Duplicate the patterns and program them with words to be alphabetized, math facts, vocabulary words and definitions, or other skills. Cut out the prepared patterns and place them in a learning center for individual practice or use them as part of a lesson.

Name ____

Dino Delivery

Read each sentence.
Write the correct blend on each envelope.
Cut out and glue each envelope to the dot on
its matching sentence.

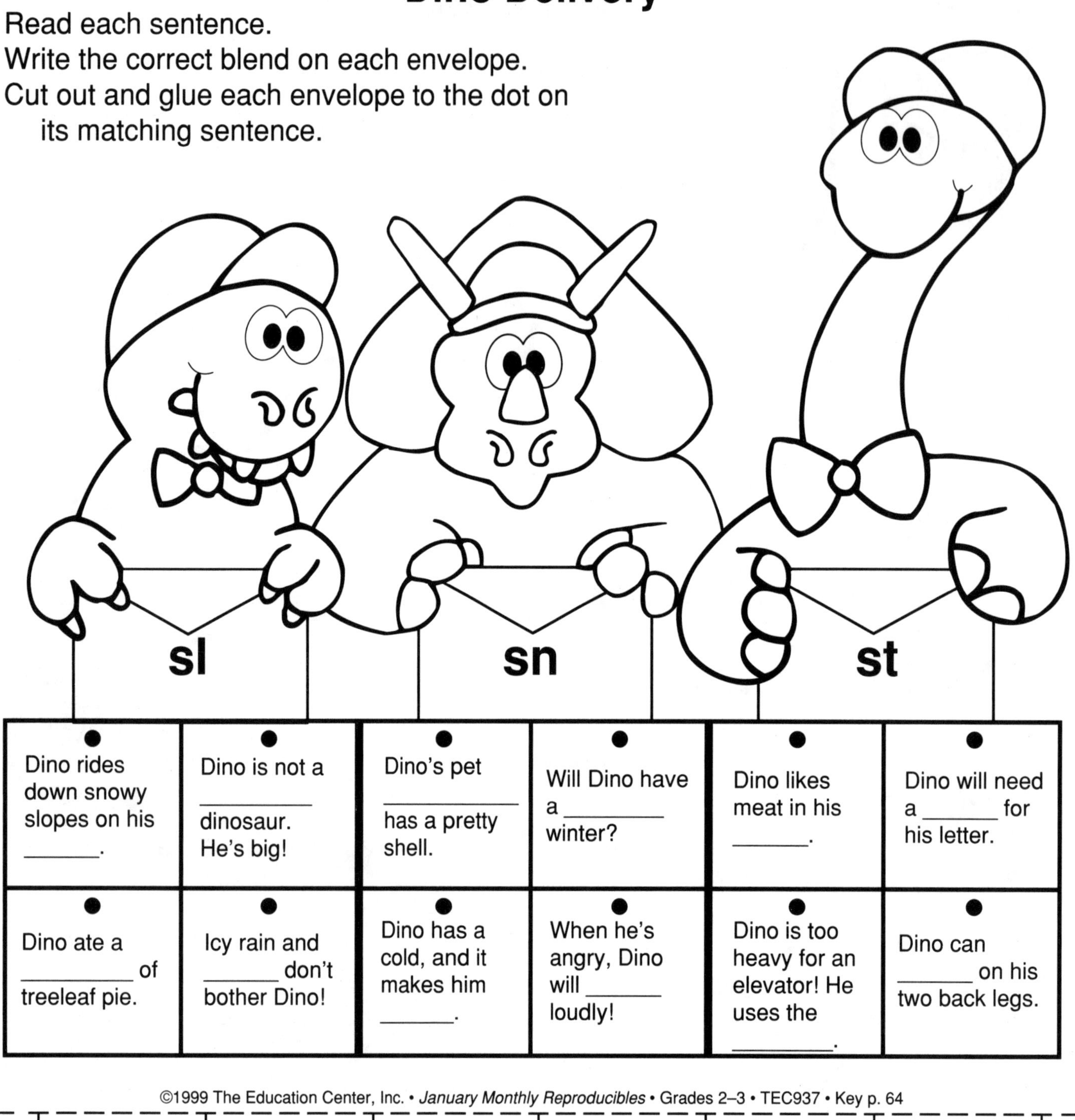

Dino rides down snowy slopes on his ______.	Dino is not a ______ dinosaur. He's big!	Dino's pet ______ has a pretty shell.	Will Dino have a ______ winter?	Dino likes meat in his ______.	Dino will need a ______ for his letter.
Dino ate a ______ of treeleaf pie.	Icy rain and ______ don't bother Dino!	Dino has a cold, and it makes him ______.	When he's angry, Dino will ______ loudly!	Dino is too heavy for an elevator! He uses the ______.	Dino can ______ on his two back legs.

___ ___ ew	___ ___ iffle	___ ___ ed	___ ___ airs	___ ___ ail	___ ___ ice
___ ___ ort	___ ___ im	___ ___ amp	___ ___ eet	___ ___ owy	___ ___ and

Name ______________________________

What's For Breakfast?

Read each sentence.
Draw hands on each clock to show the correct time.

Bonus Box: How much time does the tyrannosaurus spend hunting for his breakfast? Solve the problem on the back of this paper.

Name ____________________

Prehistoric Punctuation

Read each sentence.
Write the correct ending punctuation.
Then color a dinosaur track with the matching punctuation mark.

1. Dinosaurs lived a long time ago
2. It was a time before houses, cars, or even people
3. How long ago was it
4. It was about 65 million years ago
5. Is that before my grandparents were born
6. Yes, it was long before that
7. What kind of dinosaurs were there
8. There were some that walked on two legs and some that walked on all four
9. What did they eat
10. Some dinosaurs, such as the brachiosaurus, ate plants
11. Others, like the compsognathus, ate meat
12. Why did the dinosaurs disappear
13. There are many guesses, but no one knows for sure
14. What do you think happened to the dinosaurs

Bonus Box: On the back of this paper, write an answer to the last question.

The battle for the Super Bowl® title traditionally erupts on the last Sunday in January. Coach your young players with these math and reading activities that will spread football fever!

Going For A Field Goal!

Your youngsters will get a kick out of skills practice with this center idea! Duplicate one copy of the gameboard on page 44 and the set of game cards on page 45. Cut out the gameboard and the cards. Color the gameboard and glue it to a manila envelope. Laminate the cards and the envelope, if desired, carefully slitting the opening of the envelope with a utility knife. Next program the front of each card with a different addition or subtraction problem, and the back with its answer. Store the cards in the envelope and place the game at a learning center. To use the activity, a student removes the cards from the envelope and stacks them faceup on the gameboard. She then selects a card, works the problem on a piece of paper, and flips the card to check her answer. If she is correct, she places her card above the crossbar of the goalpost. If she is incorrect, she places it on the pile labeled "Ball Return!" When all cards have been "played," she counts the number correct so that she can try to beat her score next time. For a variation, program additional sets of cards with other math-related problems.

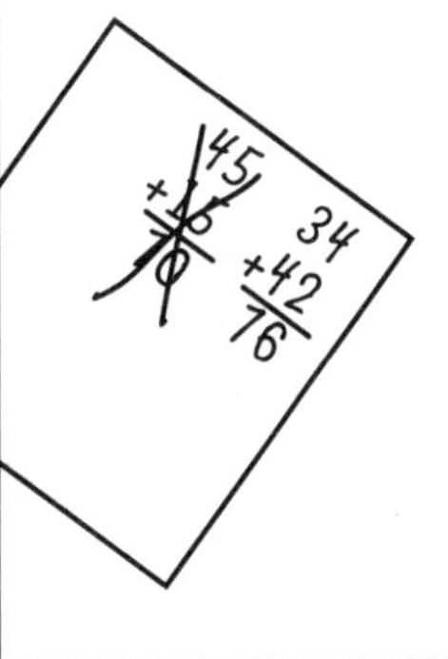

Sportscasting Fluency

Focus on reading fluency as youngsters tackle this newsworthy idea! Ahead of time, set the stage for a televised sports report. Obtain props and enlist the aid of an adult to videotape. To kick off this activity, encourage a class discussion about the traits of television sportscasters. Guide students in understanding that sportscasters speak clearly and with ease. Then announce that each student will get to play the role of sports newscaster. Give each student a copy of the script on page 46 and have students read it silently. Then ask a volunteer to read it aloud. Next direct students to work in pairs, reading each paragraph aloud several times until there is fluency. To ensure success for the less fluent readers, encourage choral readings and buddy coaching. As students become able to read the script with ease, set up the props and videotape each "newscaster" as he sits behind a desk. Once all students have been taped, show two or three sports reports a day until all have been viewed. If midyear parent conferences are scheduled, set up the video so parents can enjoy the show. Follow up with the analogies reproducible on page 47 to provide continued practice with football vocabulary. Putting fluency practice in the limelight will bring rave reviews!

Going For The Field Goal!

Kick Off! **(Place cards problem-side up.)**	**Ball Return!**

 Note To The Teacher: Use with "Going For A Field Goal!" on page 43.

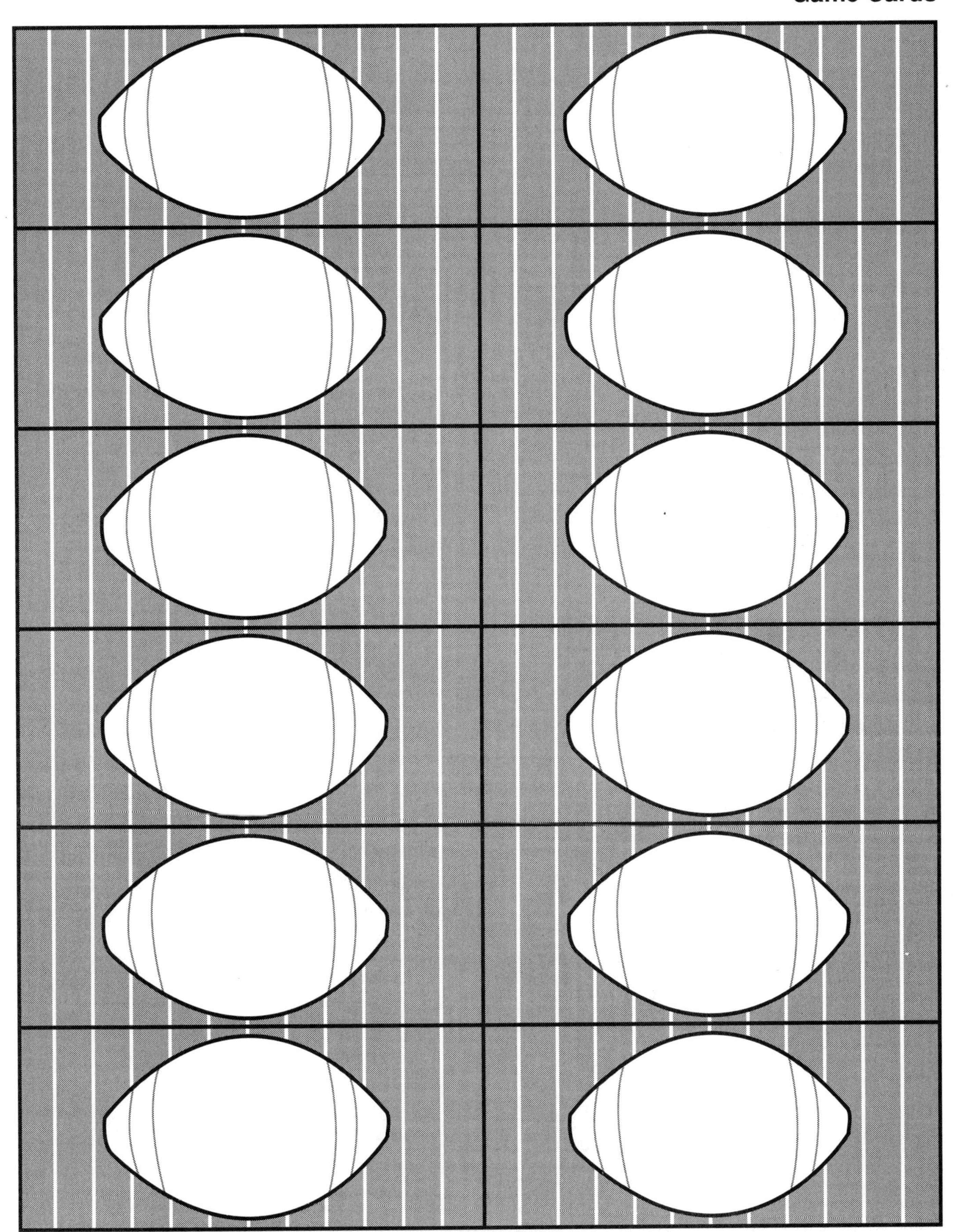

Note To The Teacher: Use with "Going For A Field Goal!" on page 43.

Name ______________________________

Welcome To The Feather Bowl, Sports Fans!

Hank Huddle here with the sports news! The Touchdown Turkeys and the Champion Chickens have been pumping up and plumping up for the year's fowlest football game—the Feather Bowl! These plucky players have also been cooking up some juicy plans for this important game!

Rumor has it that the Touchdown Turkeys nearly cooked their goose earlier this week! Instead of practicing their blocks and tackles, the team decided to have a picnic. The coaches had to round up the players and get them exercising, practicing their formations, and playing warm-up games. Those turkeys were soon soaring like eagles to catch long passes!

Today's game has gotten off to a shaky start. Why? There were no players! No coaches! No referees! Instead, the field was covered with baseball players who wanted batting practice! The mix-up was soon settled when busloads of clucking football players arrived. You should have seen the feathers fly! It wasn't long before the baseball players forgot about batting practice. They decided to join the fans in the stands and root for their favorite Feather Bowl team!

It's going to be a high-flying game today, folks! Here come our fine-feathered players onto the field now! Wow! These players look great! The Champion Chickens are dressed in their new yellow jerseys and pants. This year they even have cleats on the soles of their new shoes. I guess they won't be sliding around on the slippery field like they did last year. I see players putting on helmets, fastening chin guards, and poking beaks through face masks. They're getting ready for the kickoff now. Man, oh, man, they're strutting their drumsticks! It looks like there are going to be a lot of fowls on the field today!

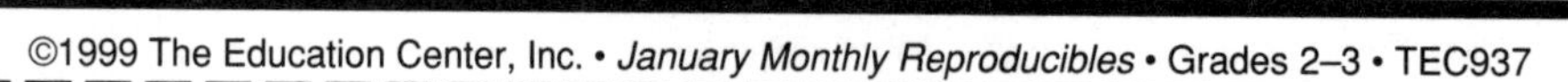

 Note To The Teacher: Use with "Sportscasting Fluency" on page 43.

Name ____

This And That

Read each group of words below.
Circle the word that does not belong.

Read the words in the helmet. Read each sentence below. On the line, write the helmet word that best completes the sentence.

baseball player
driver
shoulder
coat
hockey
coach

1. A **student** is to a **teacher** as a **football player** is to a __________.
2. **Laces** are to **shoes** as a **zipper** is to a __________.
3. A **helmet** is to a **head** as a **pad** is to a __________.
4. **Throwing** is to a **football player** as **batting** is to a __________.
5. A **field** is to **football** as an **ice rink** is to __________.
6. A **whistle** is to a **referee** as a **horn** is to a __________.

Name ____________________

Super Bowl® Kickoff
Diphthongs: ōw, ŏw

First Down

Cut out the footballs.
Read the word on each football.
Glue each football under the goalpost with the matching vowel sound.

throw

cow

grow

flown

down

snow

how

mower

brown

blow

power

crown

Bonus Box: On the back of this paper, write the words on the footballs in ABC order.

National Soup Month

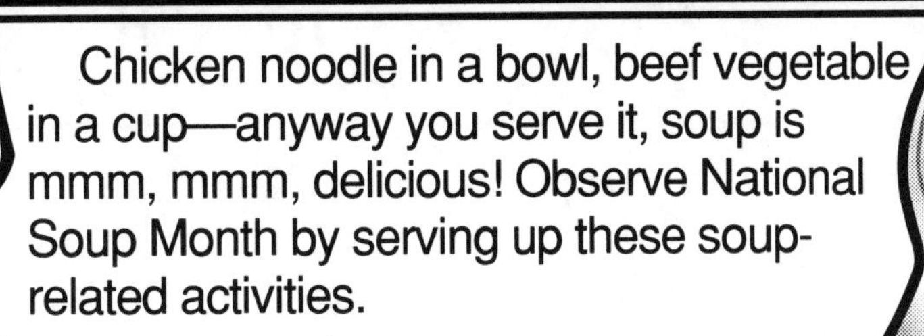

Chicken noodle in a bowl, beef vegetable in a cup—anyway you serve it, soup is mmm, mmm, delicious! Observe National Soup Month by serving up these soup-related activities.

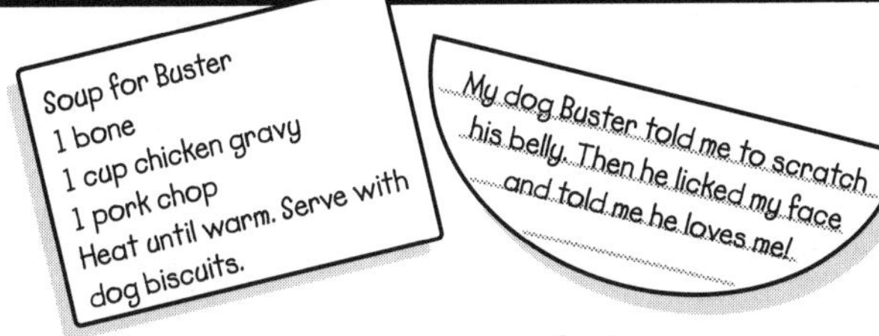

The Power Of Soup

Start with a dash of inspiration, add a pinch of imagination, and you have the beginnings of a "pet-icularly" good recipe for creative writing! For inspiration, read aloud to your class *Martha Calling* by Susan Meddaugh (Houghton Mifflin Company, 1996). This story tells about a dog that is able to talk after eating alphabet soup. Give each student an index card and a cut-out soup bowl with writing lines (see the illustration). Next ask each student to don an imaginary chef's hat. Have her write a special soup recipe for her pet or favorite animal on the index card. Instruct her to pretend that the soup gives her pet the ability to talk and have her write about her pet's experience on the cutout. Then display the recipes and soup bowls on a bulletin board titled "Soup Worth Talking About!"

"Soup-er" Math

Challenge students to use their noodles *and* their addition skills with this math center activity! Duplicate the top of page 50 onto tagboard. Cut out the boxes and, if desired, color and laminate them. Place the cards in an envelope labeled "Soup Ingredients." Next, using a permanent marker, program each of eight small plastic bowls with a different numeral from 11 to 18. Place the envelope, the bowls, and a calculator at a center. To use the center, a student selects a bowl. Then he chooses three ingredient cards that, when added together, equal the numeral on the bowl. Checking each equation with the calculator, he chooses cards until he has found as many combinations as possible. Then he chooses another bowl and continues in the same manner. What an appetizing way to practice math skills!

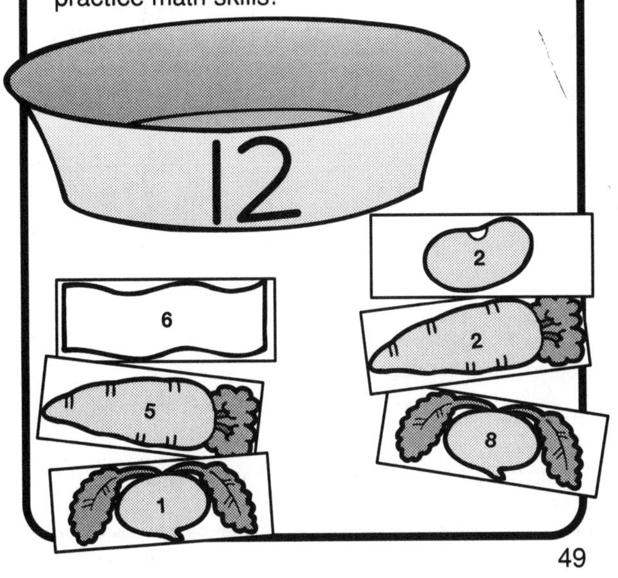

Soup's On!

Wrap up your celebration of National Soup Month with a Better-Than-Stone-Soup Party! Several days in advance, make a copy of the parent letter on page 50. Fill in each ingredient blank with a soup ingredient and send the letters home. Arrange for an adult to help supervise the cooking preparations. On the morning of the soup celebration, set up a table with one or more Crock-Pot® slow cookers, plastic bowls, spoons, and napkins. Then read aloud your favorite version of *Stone Soup* to your class. Next have each student add his ingredient to the pot. When the soup is cooked, invite students to sample it as you read *Growing Vegetable Soup* by Lois Ehlert (Harcourt Brace Jovanovich, Publishers; 1993) and *Watch Out For The Chicken Feet In Your Soup* by Tomie de Paola (Simon & Schuster Children's Division, 1985). Students will agree—one bowlful may not be enough!

Patterns

Use the ingredient cards with " 'Soup-er' Math" on page 49.
Use the parent letter with "Soup's On!" on page 49.

Ingredient Cards

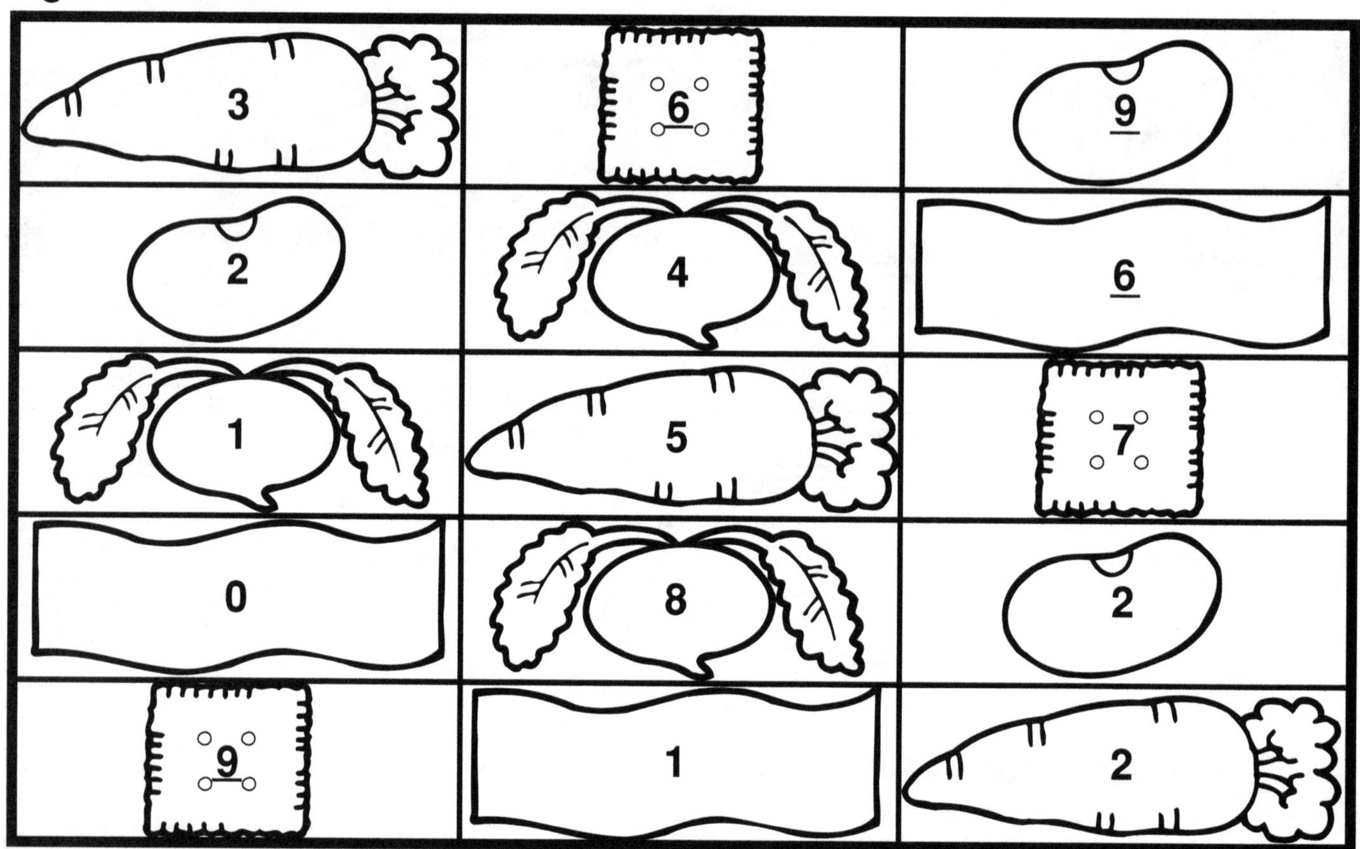

Parent Letter

Dear Family,

In celebration of National Soup Month, our class will be having our own Better-Than-Stone-Soup Party on ____________________ (Date). If you are able to contribute ______________________________ (Ingredient) to go in the soup, please complete this slip and return it to school with your child by ____________________ (Date). Thank you for your help!

____
Teacher's Signature

- -

My child, ______________________________, will bring ____________________ for the soup celebration.

____
Parent's Signature

Name ____

National Soup Month
Greater than/less than

What's Cooking?

Count the noodles in each bowl.
Write the numeral on the line.
For each pair, lightly color the bowl that has more noodles.
Write < or > in the circle to make a true statement.

Remember!
< means less than.
> means greater than.

1.	2.	3.
______ ○ ______	______ ○ ______	______ ○ ______
4.	**5.**	**6.**
______ ○ ______	______ ○ ______	______ ○ ______
7.	**8.**	**9.**
______ ○ ______	______ ○ ______	______ ○ ______

Bonus Box: The cook has 100 bowls for serving soup. Waiter Waldo has served 16 bowls of chicken noodle soup, 22 bowls of vegetable soup, and 47 bowls of split pea soup. How many clean bowls are left?

Name ____________________

Hot Stuff

Cut the boxes on the dotted lines.
Read the words on each bowl.
If the plural word is correct, glue the bowl to the tray.
If it is not correct, glue it beside the tray.

Bonus Box: Draw a line through each plural that is not correct. Then write the correct plural on its bowl.

knife knives	box boxes	spoon spoons	dish dishes	bowl bowls	chef cheves	tray trayes
potato potatoes	waiter waiters	menu menues	party parties	noodle noodles	tomato tomatos	chicken chickenes

Name ______________________________

Math Matchup

Solve each problem.
Read the soup name on the bowl.
For each spoon, find a bowl with the same answer.
Write the name on the spoon handle.

2. 36 + 26 — tomato

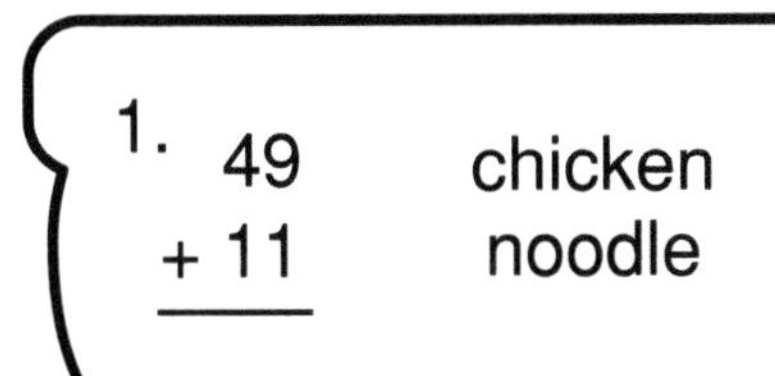

1. 49 + 11 — chicken noodle

8. 32 + 69

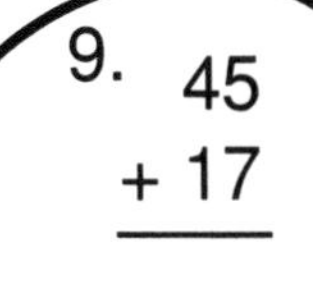

9. 45 + 17

10. 57 + 24

3. 23 + 58 — chicken and rice

4. 54 + 47 — vegetable

11. 56 + 44

12. 31 + 29

5. 16 + 17 — beef pasta

13. 29 + 16

6. 71 + 29 — potato

14. 18 + 15

7. 17 + 28 — broccoli cheese

Name ____

Soup Du Jour!

Chef Pierre was very busy during lunch today!
This graph shows the soup he sold.
Use the graph to answer the questions below.

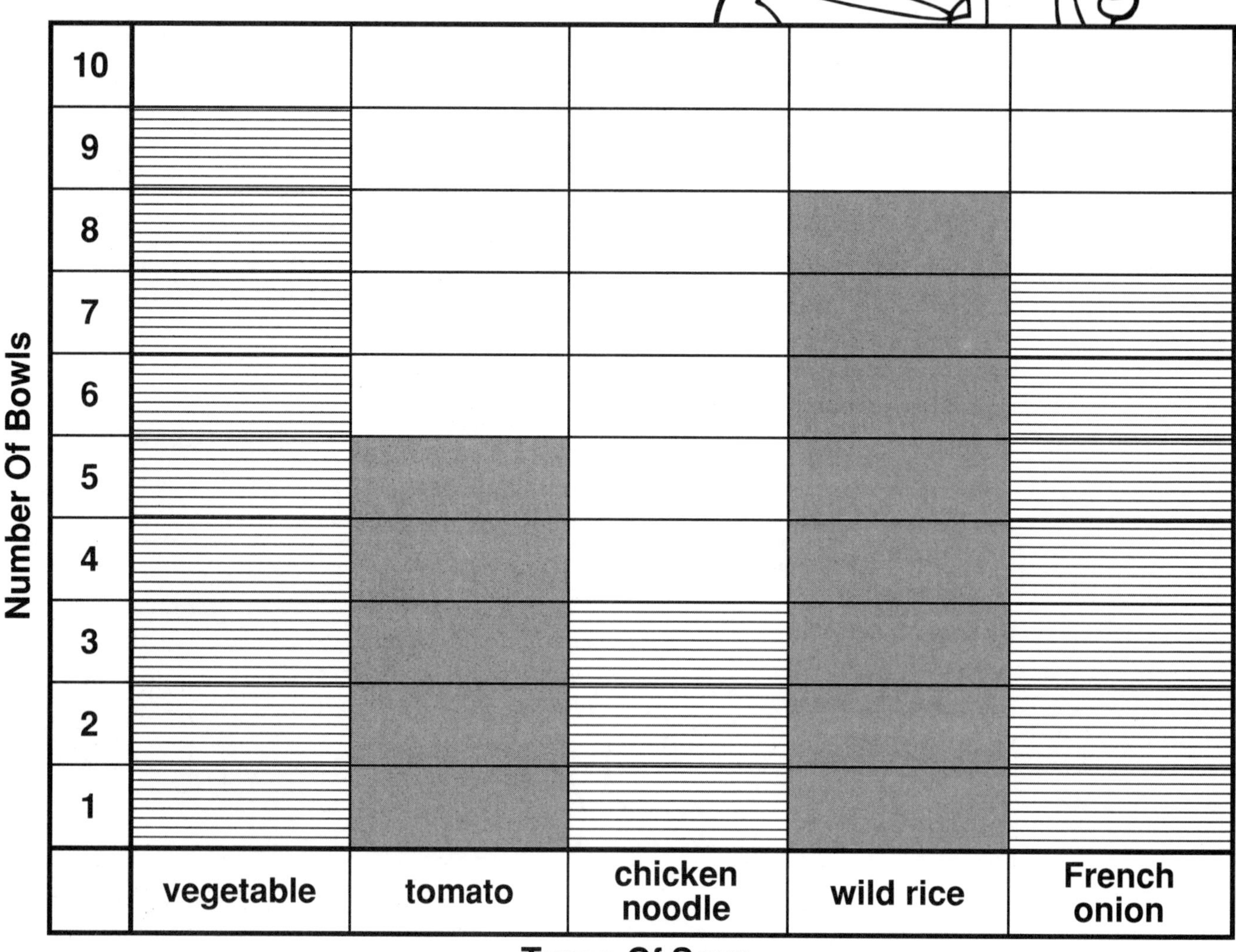

1. What soup was sold the most?_____________ The least? _______________
2. Were more bowls of tomato and chicken noodle soup sold or French onion soup?

   ____

3. How many more bowls of wild rice soup were sold than tomato soup? _________
4. How many more bowls of chicken noodle soup need to be sold to equal the amount of vegetable soup sold? ____________________
5. How many bowls of soup did Chef Pierre sell? ________________

Bonus Box: Vegetable soup costs $.10 a bowl. Chicken noodle soup costs $.25 a bowl. How much more money did Chef Pierre make selling vegetable soup? Show your work on the back of this page.

Universal Letter-Writing Week

Mail call! Here's a mailbag full of letter-writing practice for your students! Deliver this first-class unit during Universal Letter-Writing Week, January 8–14.

Fanciful Friendly Letters

Looking for a creative way for students to practice writing friendly letters? If so, try this fantastic fairy-tale idea!

Read aloud to students your favorite version of *Little Red Riding Hood.* Discuss with youngsters each character's personality traits and his or her role in the story. Write the name of each character on a different paper strip; then place the strips in a container. Next assign each student a partner. In turn, have each twosome take two prepared strips from the container and read aloud the names. Then ask the youngsters to return the strips to the container for the next student pair. Give each student a copy of page 56 and review the parts of a friendly letter. Instruct each youngster to write a letter to his partner's character from the perspective of his own character. Have partners exchange and read the letters. Then instruct each student to respond to the letter he received on another copy of page 56. Display students' work on a bulletin board titled "Special Delivery." Now that's a letter-perfect idea to improve letter-writing *and* character-analysis skills!

Amazing Addresses

Reinforce envelope addressing skills with this "send-sational" center! To prepare, cut 30 strips of paper. Label each of the first ten strips with a different fairy-tale or story character's name. Write a different fictional street address on each of the next ten strips. Then label each of the remaining strips with a different city, state abbreviation, and fictional zip code. To make the activity self-checking, write "1," "2," or "3" on the back of each strip to correspond with its position in an address. Store each set of strips in a labeled envelope. Place the labeled envelopes in a center along with a supply of pencils, blank letter-size envelopes, and a container to represent a mailbox. As needed, review with students how to address envelopes before they visit the center.

To use the center, a student selects a strip from each labeled envelope. She sequences the strips to create a complete address. The youngster continues in a like manner with the remaining strips until she has made ten addresses. After she has checked her work, the student chooses her favorite address and writes it on a blank envelope. She writes her actual return address and draws a stamp. Then the student places her envelope in the mailbox. After several envelopes have been addressed and placed in the mailbox, extend the activity by asking students to sort the envelopes by name, street address, or state. Then have them create a class graph to show the results.

Snow White
121 Charming Court
Nome, AK 12345

First-Class Literature

Dear Peter Rabbit by Alma Flor Ada (Simon & Schuster Children's Division, 1997)
Felix Travels Back In Time by Annette Langen (Abbeville Kids, 1995)
The Jolly Postman Or Other People's Letters by Janet & Allan Ahlberg (Little, Brown And Company; 1986)
Where Does The Mail Go? by Melvin & Gilda Berger (Ideals Children's Books, 1994)
Toot & Puddle by Holly Hobbie (Little, Brown And Company; 1997)

 Note To The Teacher: Use with “Fanciful Friendly Letters” on page 55.

Name ______________________

Wolfy's Friendly Letter

Cut out the strips on the dotted lines.
Read the strips. Place them in order.
Glue each strip in the correct space on the letter.
Use the color code to outline each part of the letter.

Color Code:

date = purple **greeting** = orange
body = blue **closing** = red
signature = green

sorry if I scared you. I would like to be

friends with you. See you tomorrow!

I am so glad that I met you! I'm very

January 16, 2000	Dear Little Red Riding Hood,
Wolfy	Your friend,

Name ____

Sincerely Yours

Read Little Red Riding Hood's letter.
Use the proofreading marks to correct her letter.
Each time you make a correction, color a matching footprint.

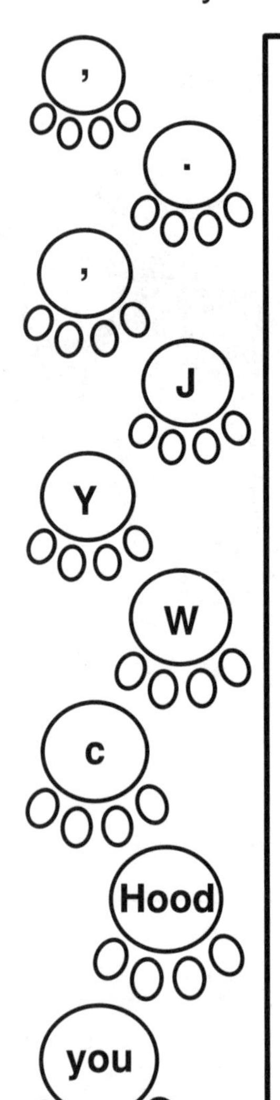

january 18 2000

dear mr. Woodcutter

Thank very much for your Help.

i was so scared My grandmother and I

are very lucky that were nearby.

would you like to have tea and cookies

with us tomorrow My grandmother bakes the

best Cookies! They are delicious. I hope to

see you soon

your Friend,

Little red Riding

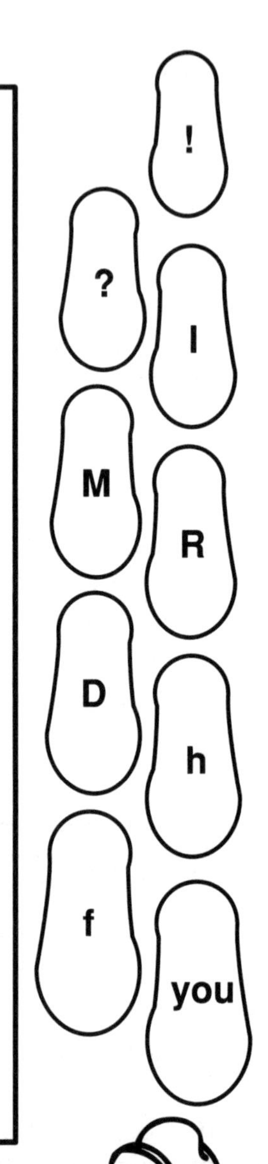

Proofreading Marks

Change to a capital letter.	D (over) did you stay on the path? (≡ under d)
Change to a lowercase letter.	She Carried the basket of food. (C crossed out, c above)
Add missing punctuation.	Grandma was sick.
Add a word.	She was ^ a red outfit. (wearing inserted)

Bonus Box: On the back of this sheet, write Mr. Woodcutter's answer to this letter. Remember to proofread your work.

Hooray For Pooh Day!

Hundred Acre Wood is pulsing with excitement! What's the occasion? It's January 18—Pooh Day—which celebrates the birthdate of Pooh's much beloved creator, A. A. Milne. Celebrate the adventures of that "silly old Bear" with these engaging language arts, social studies, and math activities.

Character Sticks

This retelling activity is sure to please your little bears! After sharing one of your favorite Winnie-the-Pooh stories, ask youngsters to name the characters in the story and list their responses on the chalkboard. Then pair students. Give each pair a white construction-paper copy of page 60. Instruct youngsters to color and cut out the characters, then glue each character to a different craft stick. Invite students to use the character sticks to retell Pooh stories. If desired, have students retell their stories to a kindergarten class. What a "bear-y" fun way to share a story!

The Many Adventures Of Pooh

Challenge youngsters to create new adventures for Pooh. Read aloud several Pooh stories to students. After sharing, have students brainstorm new adventures for Pooh and his friends. Write students' responses on a sheet of chart paper. Then provide each child with a copy of the pattern on page 61. Direct each student to choose one adventure from the brainstormed list. Have each student write and illustrate a Pooh adventure on her pattern. Then instruct her to cut out her pattern, glue it to a slightly larger sheet of brown construction paper, and trim the paper to create a border. Provide time for each youngster to share her story with classmates. Then display the stories on a bulletin board titled "The Many New Adventures Of Winnie-The-Pooh!" There's a bulletin board that will be one in a "Milne-ion!"

Hundred Acre Map

This small-group activity is just what you need to review mapping skills. Referring to the inside front cover of *Winnie-The-Pooh,* draw a simple map of Hundred Acre Wood on the chalkboard. Encourage discussion about the details of the land, such as the pit where Roo plays and the boggy area. Next divide students into groups of four. Provide each group with a sheet of poster board, clay, and a variety of construction paper. Have each group use the clay to create a map of Hundred Acre Wood including trees and streams. Challenge them to use construction paper to add features, such as signs for Pooh's home. Instruct each group to create a compass rose and key for its map. Display the maps around the room. Now that's hands-on learning!

Patterns
Use with "Character Sticks" on page 59.

Pattern

Use with "The Many Adventures Of Pooh" on page 59.

Name____________________

Do The Pooh Skip!

Complete the pattern for each row.
Then, on the line, write a sentence that explains what the pattern is.

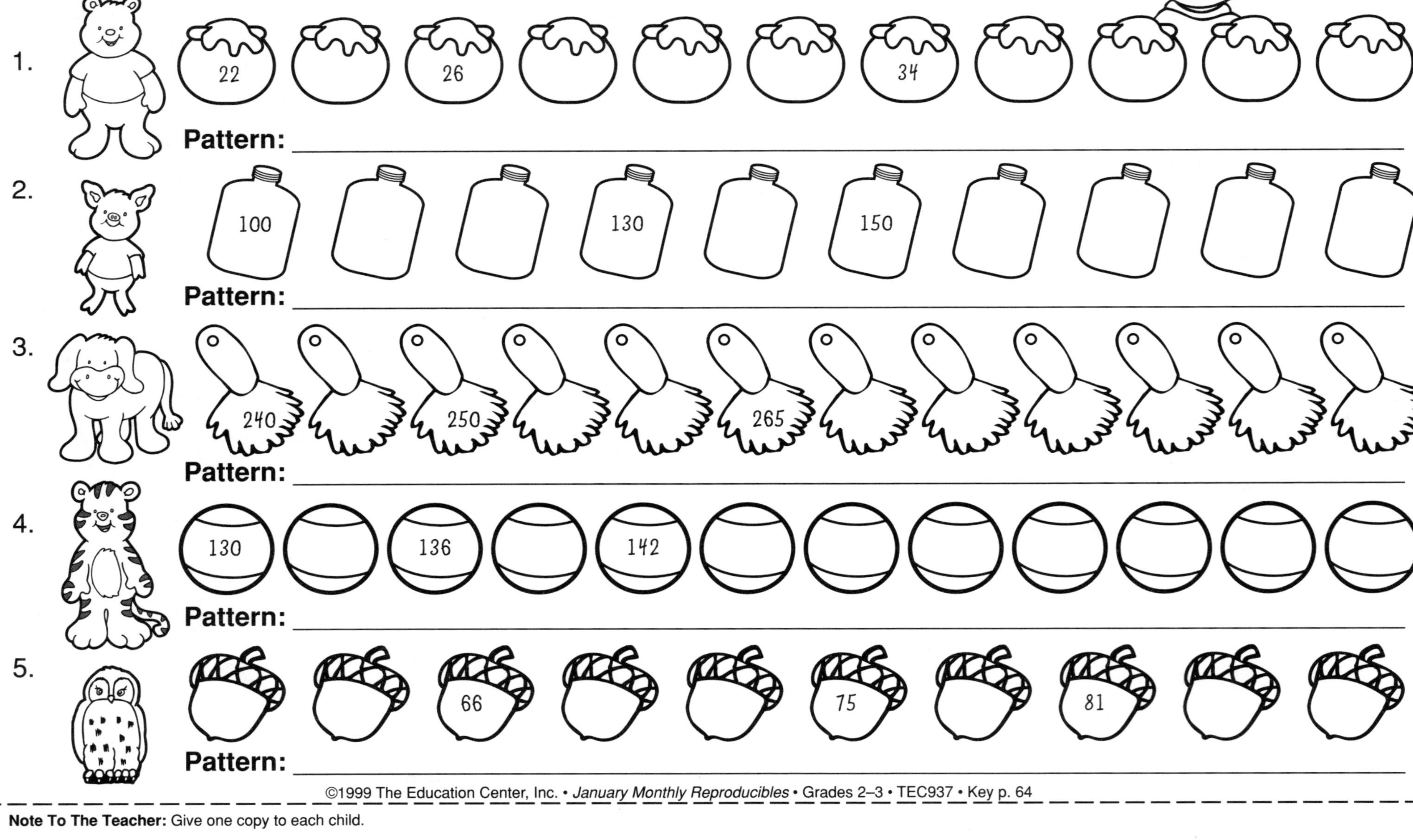

1. Pattern: ____________________

2. Pattern: ____________________

3. Pattern: ____________________

4. Pattern: ____________________

5. Pattern: ____________________

Note To The Teacher: Give one copy to each child.

Answer Keys

Page 9
Bonus Box:
1. $.65
2. $.71
3. $.42
4. $.37
5. $.82
6. $.26
7. $.34
8. $.13
9. $.23
10. $.01

Page 10
When the place values are glued in the correct balloons, the message will read "Have a cool new year!"

Page 14
1. opinion
2. fact
3. fact
4. opinion
5. opinion
6. fact
7. fact
8. opinion
9. fact
10. opinion

Page 22
1. polar sea
2. taiga
3. taiga
4. tundra
5. polar sea
6. tundra
7. polar sea
8. tundra

Page 23
1. doorway
2. playground
3. flashlight
4. strawberry
5. sunshine
6. cupcake
7. outside
8. junkyard
9. airplane
10. baseball

Page 24
1. 381
2. 723
3. 860
4. 819
5. 791
6. 705
7. 690
8. 950
9. 453
10. 625
11. 365
12. 878
13. 917
14. 829
15. 221

Page 28
beak
bird
black
chilly
cold
waddle
white
winter

feathers
fish
flippers
ice
igloo
swimmer
water
wing

Page 29
1. ~~20~~, 19 balloons
2. ~~2~~, 11 sandwiches
3. ~~2~~, 14 penguins
4. ~~2~~, 17 prizes
5. ~~10~~, 6 pictures
6. ~~11~~, 18 songs
7. ~~3~~, 14 things to sit on
8. ~~6~~, 16 colored hats

Page 30
1. ate
2. eight
3. whole
4. hole
5. knew
6. new
7. way
8. weigh
9. won
10. one
11. see
12. sea

Bonus Box: too, two
by, bye
be
so

Page 35
1. T
2. F
3. T
4. F
5. F
6. T
7. T
8. F
9. F

A new invention starts with an <u>idea</u>.

Page 36
S = 23
L = 26
A = 48
R = 29
N = 7
D = 49
K = 16
P = 47
W = 24
G = 37
O = 8
H = 79
I = 54
E = 28
T = 38

GLOW-IN-THE-DARK "REP-TILES"

Answer Keys

Page 40
Dino rides down snowy slopes on his **sled**.
Dino is not a **slim** dinosaur. He's big!
Dino ate a **slice** of treeleaf pie.
Icy rain and **sleet** don't bother Dino!

Dino's pet **snail** has a pretty shell.
Will Dino have a **snowy** winter?
Dino has a cold, and it makes him **sniffle**.
When he's angry, Dino will **snort** loudly!

Dino likes meat in his **stew**.
Dino will need a **stamp** for his letter.
Dino is too heavy for an elevator! He uses the **stairs**.
Dino can **stand** on his two back legs.

Page 41
Bonus Box: 5 hours and 25 minutes

Page 42
1. **.**
2. **.**
3. **?**
4. **.**
5. **?**
6. **.**
7. **?**
8. **.**
9. **?**
10. **.**
11. **.**
12. **?**
13. **.**
14. **?**

Page 47
1. jersey
   pants
   team
   shoes
2. helmet
   football
   cake
   field
3. window
   blocking
   tackling
   catching
4. players
   coaches
   pilots
   referees
5. practice
   baseball
   exercise
   play
6. helmet
   shoes
   chin guard
   face mask
7. shoelaces
   soles
   cleats
   shoulder pad
8. ice skating
   football
   baseball
   soccer

1. coach
2. coat
3. shoulder
4. baseball player
5. hockey
6. driver

Page 48

throw	**cow**
grow	down
flown	how
snow	brown
mower	power
blow	crown

Bonus Box: blow, brown, crown, down, flown, grow, how, mower, power, snow

Page 51
1. 15 > 12
2. 7 < 9
3. 9 < 10
4. 14 > 10
5. 16 >11
6. 13 < 15
7. 10 > 9
8. 8 > 6
9. 8 < 11

Bonus Box: 15 clean bowls

Page 53
8. 101; vegetable
9. 62; tomato
10. 81; chicken and rice
11. 100; potato
12. 60; chicken noodle
13. 45; broccoli cheese
14. 33; beef pasta

Page 54
1. the most: vegetable
   the least: chicken noodle
2. tomato and chicken noodle
3. 3 bowls
4. 6 bowls
5. 32 bowls

Bonus Box: $.15

Page 62
1. 22, **24,** 26, **28, 30, 32,** 34, **36, 38, 40, 42**
   The pattern is counting by 2s.
2. 100, **110, 120,** 130, **140,** 150, **160, 170, 180, 190**
   The pattern is counting by 10s.
3. 240, **245,** 250, **255, 260,** 265, **270, 275, 280, 285, 290, 295**
   The pattern is counting by 5s.
4. 130, **133,** 136, **139,** 142, **145, 148, 151, 154, 157, 160, 163**
   The pattern is counting by 3s.
5. **60, 63,** 66, **69, 72,** 75, **78,** 81, **84, 87**
   The pattern is counting by 3s.